***WARNI

This book contains potentially triggering content in the areas of abuse (physically, mentally, emotionally, and sexually)

TABLE OF CONTENTS

Dedication 1

Preface 2

Ch 1: Ending Generational Curses 6

Ch 2: Next Destination – Fight or Flight 45

Ch 3: A Problem or the Problem? 67

Ch 4: Picking Up the Torch 84

Ch 5: Walking In Your Truth 87

Ch 6: The New Destination 95

About the Author 105

Miracle Child

"THERE IS NO SUCH THING AS A LOST CAUSE, ONLY A WORK IN PROGRESS"

Arial D. Harper

Published by Lee's Press and Publishing Company
www.LeesPress.net

A Premiere Self-Publishing Services Company

All rights reserved 2024, Except for brief excerpts for review purposes, no part of this book may be reproduced or used in any form without written permission from Arial D. Harper and/or the publisher.

This document is published by Lee's Press and Publishing Company located in the United States of America. It is protected by the United States Copyright

Act, all applicable state laws, and international copyright laws. The information in this document is accurate to the best of the ability of Arial D. Harper at the time of writing. The content of this document is subject to change without notice.

ISBN-13: 978-1-964234-05-2

Paperback

DEDICATION

"A dedication to the inner child that experienced their first loss when they lost their voice and became powerless along the way losing themselves."

PREFACE

It was a frigid night. I couldn't tell if it was really the weather that night or the fact that in the next few hours, I was going to be in a living nightmare. My worst nightmare!

I sat beside my mother's bed in the crisp hollow hospital room that night, taking deep, anxious breaths as I watched her battle for her life. She had always been tough, and gorgeous, I must add. Even in ill health, her beauty remained, only dented by scars from her sickbed— the paleness in her skin and weakness in her eyes.

I watched my mother closely as she summoned all the strength in her to let three words slip out inaudibly from her breath just before she cried what would become her last cry. Three words she hardly ever said, "*I...am...sorry*", her last three words before she breathed her last.

I'll be honest; before this night, I had gotten so good at being numb about things, so much that most people actually started to believe I didn't care about anything at all. But they were just about to understand that I was only a silent storm brewing for a really long time.

With all the rage in me, I screamed! Loud enough to get the attention of people in the hospital's garage, meters away from my mother's ward. From my voice, one could tell that a well of pain and regret had opened up in my heart. From it flowed all my tears, I cried for hours.

This was an end, but, quite ironically, a beginning. I saw my mother leave my life forever, but as I watched her lay lifeless on the hospital bed that moment, I could no longer carry all my baggage, hold back my tears, or pretend I didn't care. I could no longer pretend that my traumas had never happened. I felt like a door had been opened, and for the first time in a long time, I had actually felt something other than anger or rage that night. It was an emotion that I couldn't explain.

Images of what my life had been like in the past years flashed in my memory all at once; the times when my innocence was stripped from me again and again to the point where it felt like I didn't have any left, being beaten time and time again physically, mentally and emotionally, "You're nothing", "You will be in jail before you're 19", "It's all your fault"— words that seeped into my ears from the very lips that were supposed to keep me safe and love me.

I, at that moment, began to see her last three words as a necessary end; an apology for all the chaos, and a life-altering end that ushered in the beginning of my healing journey. I grabbed my mother's hand as I sulked loudly, and as I let her go, I let it all go with her with an apology no matter how loud, I feel that could never be heard again.

'SCARS'. How much do you want to bet that every person in this world has one somewhere on their body, A blemish? A bump? Or hidden internally?

I believe that one way or another, we all possess some sort of imperfection that creates a narrative in our minds about ourselves. Even the ones with the most flawless skin, long pretty hair, and the presentation of having it all together have these. These bruises, scars and imperfections are beyond what others see, sometimes hidden in our stories. My name is **Danielle Love Jones**, and I am just about to share mine.

With a name like LOVE, you would think mine's a love story, but this is instead a story of hurt, abuse, neglect and of course, redemption and survival.

Before I begin, let's create two fairly simple rules for ourselves.

<u>Rule 1</u>: Admire your scars for once instead of avoiding them. <u>Rule 2</u>: Say your truth out loud that you have tried your whole life to forget or cover up like a model on a hot Saturday night.

Remember; these rules will come in handy because it is my desire that after reading this book, we will never come back to our baggage because we want to continue our intimate relationship with pain, but only revisit them as reminders of progress on the healing journey. My sole objective is that your life experiences a 360 change. How do you treat a person who has a fresh injury? Do you close the wound and ignore it, or would you disinfect and dress it appropriately? The latter would seem to be a better option. Your failure to treat that wound will get it infected. That's what happens to a lot of bleeding hearts; they ignore their wounds, and so it gets infected. An infected wound only makes things worse. This is the same for any emotional injury.

I enjoy freedom today because I've released myself from the shackles of my past. I had to come to terms with what had happened to me. I had to tell myself that as horrid as those things were, it doesn't define me. This will be my release from the prison I have lived in since

I took my first breath and breath of fresh air for you. I am not my past and you aren't yours too. Together, let's live free and never let anything or anyone ever confine us into a life sentence.

Since you know how my story ends, I guess it's time to take you to the beginning. Not just my beginning, but the actual beginning!

CHAPTER 1

ENDING GENERATIONAL CURSES

"People get stuck on a hamster wheel when it come to their ways because they have only seen those ways their entire life."
- A.H

The shrill cry of a child echoes down the hall of the hospital, and everybody celebrates its birth. Babies are the cutest things on earth; you just want to cuddle them endlessly. Having a child also opens up your heart to a new dimension of love you have never experienced—the unique love between parents and their children. This is such an unbreakable bond; you will never know you could love another human being like that until you have a child. So, the one thing parents try to do is to protect their children from harm. They often try to look out for them in every way that they can, and to shield them from the harsh realities of this world. But as much as they try, a parent cannot hundred percent protect their child from harm—well, unless they are thinking of locking them in a glass pod where they cannot interact with the outside world. This seems like something straight out of a sci-fi movie.

Although I believe that no parent can truly protect their child(ren) from harm, I think they can at least try to protect them from walking the same dark paths or through the same dark doors they had walked in their life. Life presents parenting as a chance to redo all that went wrong in your own life, and most importantly do better for your children. It is a chance to make sure that your children do not go through the same things you had been through. When I think about it this way, I realize that this is why my mother would think that her last three words were what I wanted to hear from her. The reality of her words hit me—she felt like she had failed me. It was her chance to hold me back from walking the same dark doors she had walked through, that her parents had let her walk through...but, she threw it all away! And so, my life went on, diligently adhering to a cycle.

I had some time to think about it a little more, about what my mother could have done better, and one question haunted my mind: *Can one truly give what they do not have or had not been given?* Or put differently, **how does one teach what they had not been taught?**

My mother, Rose Linda Jones, had me at the age of 29—the prime of her life. This was a time when she was still practically trying to figure out what life even meant. She was born in a rather small and close-knit community in Arkansas, Louisville, Arkansas. This place, for my mother was a personal prison most days.

Her parents, Marie Grantfield and Nick Joe Jones came from two completely different backgrounds. Gramma Marie was a petite quiet woman. Even though, she was a woman of few words, she had a heart full of gold for everyone. I only remember the story of my grandmother as a tragic story. From not knowing her father, to her mother giving her and her 5 siblings away at an early age, and basically being raised from house to house with whomever would take her in.

My grandfather on the other hand, was a handsome southern gentleman, notorious for his radiant smile, city-slicker style in clothes and his way with words in all that he encountered. I feel like he could have talked a baby out of a sucker and a mother out of being mad about it too. He came from a very wealthy family that prided themselves in religion, family, and service to others. One would think he was a giant, if they were to hold my grandmother in comparison, but height and body build didn't matter where love was. These two shared a common love for being each other's strengths in their weaknesses. Everything was rosy, until then, it was not.

Marie's upbringing had taught her to be scared of the world. We would come to agree that in truth, the environment we grow up in and the abuse we endure shapes our mind-set, and this in turn affects the choices we make in life. Marie's fears would ultimately lead to the end of their relationship, but not until they birthed a beautiful baby girl who they named Rose—my mother.

Together, they tried to raise their daughter. But the reality of parenting with varying backgrounds, is that it becomes a challenging on what values to instil in your child and which patterns to follow. This puts the child at the center of the conflict.

My grandfather Nick often spent little or no time at home—not so much of a comfort for a nursing mother. Marie needed him, and the longer he stayed away from home, the more strained their relationship became. A lurking disaster.

"Why are you gone all the time Nick?" my grandmother will always holler. "Even while you're here, why can't we spend time as a family?"

It became a daily routine, the order of their home. If Gramma Marie wasn't yelling at Nick for not being home, it was about changing their daughter Rose. It got worse, from consistent arguments to no arguments at all. *How does that make it worse? Well, Nick disappeared.*

Rose was only four months old, when Nick eventually decided to find love in the arms of another woman. And like you would expect, he walked out of their lives—Rose's and Marie's, to be with his new wife, never to be heard from or seen for a really long while.

Peace! You will think. I see you assuming that Nick's impromptu exit will give Marie a chance to start afresh, with the right person perhaps. Or, maybe, even fix things somehow. But contrary to what you may think, this moment right here, is what I would rather define as "The Beginning of the Curse".

Rose grew up to be a beautiful young girl; slim and slender body almost like her mother's, beautiful brown hair, with eyes that charmed when she smiled. Her smile, there was really something about it. Just like her father, this seemed to get her into trouble a lot.

She was athletic, with a bubbly, outspoken personality almost too big for where she came from. You could bet she had everything, but an ideal home.

Rose was shown love, at least in the way she understood love to be. For her and her younger brother Pete, love often looked like screaming, hollering, belittling, and being beaten into submission.

When Nick left, Marie's life was thrown in chaos. And for someone who had no background or clue on proper parenting, treating her little kids as mini adults was okay. In this way, her children were exposed to alcohol and drinking at the age of six; they would often return from school to a can of beer waiting for them in the car.

How could she have known better, or from whom?

What mattered most to Marie was that she was taking care of her children as the law demanded—it didn't matter how well. With no father figure and a ...mother, Rose and her brother were forced to grow up in a completely dysfunctional home. Now where Rose had become immune to most situation her younger brother Pete was quite the opposite. My uncle Pete has a very small part in my story but the biggest impact the way most people would never imagine. As a kid he was the "cool kid" on the block that was known in the community for being Marie's son but also because of his heart with others. His normal days in his teenage years was playing basketball in the community or going to the local juke joint to play pool with his friends. He stood 5'9, slim, with a part in his head with a box cut that made most girls flock to him especially when he smiled. While his life may not have always been perfect from stories, I was told I later recognized that he was good at putting good people in his life to escape some of his wounds along the way. I have always had the thought some people enlist into the military because it is a familiar form of abuse. In my eyes that's the reason I feel that Uncle Pete enlisted and never turned back because honestly, what did he really have to lose besides sanity? I don't think it was a time that he didn't love his family but it's often hard to find love when pain is the source of every memory. Surprisingly when I grew up, he turned out to be someone that knew my heart better than anyone even in the places that I don't often read out loud. It's funny as I write this because everyone told stories about how we were so attached to each other when I was a baby, and I don't think my heart ever forgot the love I felt from him in all these years. Now that you know a piece about my Uncle Pete now back to the story at hand.

A woman's beauty almost never fades.

Years went by, but even time was not enough to stop Marie from catching the eye of another—Clark Green. Marie would fall deeply in love, without no knowledge that she is about to experience a familiar version of love in the arms of this psychopath.

****

Clark Green seemed to be the exact opposite of my grandfather Nick, visually and internally. He was very slender, with a gold tooth on his right front tooth, and a signature scent that I can still remember like a tick on my skin. He smelled of after shave and wintergreen alcohol. Clark was much older than Marie, but they seemed to come from similar traumatic backgrounds and this kind of equated them mentally. Clark came from a family of alcoholics and thieves—borderline dysfunctional family. This to Marie, was normal in her world.

When Marie and Clark first got together, they had house parties all the time. Grammar Marie was an incredible cook, and often complemented her amazing cooking skills with drinking, and listening to Blues—every single one known to man. Marie and Clark would often invite the neighbours over to eat and have fun under the lights in the carport that seemed much more like a hidden juke joint, than what it really was.

Booze and lighting on airy evenings sets the perfect stage for excitement; the feeling of being wild and free. It was normal to overdo and pass out on such nights. Was this truly fun? Or an alternative method to sending the pain away.

Parties after parties led to a wedding party. Now they were married, she was locked with visiting her juke joint for life, what seemed to be her safe space. But what Marie failed to realize was that every night she spent there, she stole a valuable night off her children's life. Her children, where were they on these nights?

My mother Rose and her brother Pete were often left in the care of themselves. Well, on some nights. On others, Rose was summoned outside to 'share in the fun' perhaps, but only when the party was over. Clark would beckon on Rose to sit on his laps and watch him play cards. Naive Rose, who was only rather elated to have a father figure back in her life would jump on Clark's lap like that was all that mattered. And whenever he whispered the prey question "Do you really love me?" into the little girl's ear, she would grin the widest and reply in excitement "Yes, I do".

****

It was one of those nights. The adults had finished playing their games in the make-do junkie joint with everyone highly intoxicated from the alcohol and smoke. Marie had managed to stagger herself to her room leaving Rose outside with Clark.

With people leaving, the entire place was soon empty, and it was just about time for Clark to strike.

"Tell me Rose, do you really love me?" Clark whispered as he caressed Rose's hair, his breath reeking of cigarettes and Budweiser.

Rose's eyes gleamed, and her lips twitched in a smile, "Yes...yes I do" she echoed excitedly.

"Oh, you sure do..." he teased, this time tickling her with his fingers "I know you do..."

Rose laughed hard as she wriggled her body, making sure he hadn't tickled the same spot twice. A six-year-old enjoying the cool of the night, under the roof of her 'step-father's love'. Or so her little, clueless mind thought.

"Okay love, you should go get in bed. You've got school in the morning" Clark finally stopped playing.

With a nod, Rose jumped right out of Clark's laps and hurriedly made her way to her room to undress and get into bed. With this excitement—the excitement of finally spending time with a father, she was definitely going to have a good sleep.

The cold wind that blew in through Rose's window made it easier for her to get comfortable and start dozing off. But then, she was startled by a noise in the hallway.

I she lifted up her head and listened more closely in the noise's direction, she could decipher that they were footsteps. This wasn't unusual, being that the toilet was on the other end of the hallway. But for some reason, this night, Rose was extremely frightened. She clenched her blanket fiercely as she laid back down, waiting to hear if the footsteps would end, but it stopped right in front of her door. The shadowy figure walked into the light, to reveal it was Clark.

"Hey, baby" he whispered as he staggered closer to her bed, drunk as ever. "I came in here to make sure you came and got in the bed".

As he smiled, his gold tooth twinkled in the fairly bright room. This made the whole scene look even more scary and mischievous. Rose pulled up her blanket again, hogging it more tightly than before.

He found a spot to sit on the bed "Do you love me, Rose?"

Rose, wondering why her stepfather kept asking her a question she had already given answers to, nodded her head in fear. The man placed his both hands on her shoulders, and slowly and gently, began to rub them.

"Then show me you love me".

For a moment, he stopped. Then pulled Rose closer as he reached for her clothes to take them off, Rose obliging somewhat reluctantly.

"You loved the tickles, didn't you?", he took off her blouse "I'm just making sure you feel the tickles".

As Clark started to kiss Rose, the little girl began to get uncomfortable.

"No, stop, please" she begged till she began to cry. But Clark was too intoxicated and invested to hear a thing.

It was probably why he never noticed Pete watching at the door. Pete had just returned from using the bathroom, and when he noticed unusual sounds in Rose's he stood at the door and watched in fear.

Rose, too brittle to fight off an adult man, began to grow weaker and weaker the more she struggled. So, Clark proceeded to have his way, making sure he devoured every bit of Rose's innocence.

"Please stop!! LET ME GOOO please!!!" her scream echoed in the hallway.

Pete could no longer stay quiet. He picked up an umbrella from the side of the door and rushed into the scene, landing the object on Clark's back with a hard hit. Clark's attention was drawn to his attacker.

"You little.... thing" he roared as he reached to grab the boy's hand. This gave Rose little time to free herself enough to grab a pillow.

"Stop, Go away! Help!" she continued to scream.

The commotion had finally gotten to Marie's ears, she hurried to the scene.

"He was over me mom! He wouldn't stop" Rose's tears intensified as soon as she had sighted her mother at the door.

Marie quickly made her way further into the room and held Clark back from hitting Pete.

"She must be kiddin' yeah?" she muttered almost inaudibly "What are they saying about you having sex with Rose?"

Clark remained silent, only panting hard. Saying nothing about his silence and without expecting a response, Marie turned the anger on her children.

"And you two.... what you doin' up when y'all should be in bed?"

Strictly to Rose this time, she yelled "You were playing outside after I went to bed, you think you can break the rules huh?"

Rose was startled the more. One would think that a mother hen would fight a hawk for trying to prey on her chick, and not on her chick for being preyed on. But you would guess Gramma Marie never got the memo.

"Get outta here" Clark's voice echoed as he pushed Marie away. "You've got no business here. Stay outta this".

"But..." she tried to say, when she felt her head hit against the wall. A slap followed.

"You try to get in my way, you get punished for it, you hear me?"

That was it that night. Marie wailed as Clark beat her round their over 200sq ft home. For Marie, this was the beginning of yet another tragic story.

*****

From that night until my mother Rose was twelve years old, she was raped by Clark, and nobody ever said a word to him about it.

My grandmother Marie on several accounts stated she didn't say anything out of fear that he would start to hit her. I would understand that Marie had been scared of people all her life, but when I think about it now, was that really the only option? Who was to save; herself from being abused, or her child? Why would one want love if love hurts so bad and comes with so much fear?

A time came when my grandmother kicked my mother out of the house, and again, there are so many questions that surround the reasons why she did. Was it to protect my mother? Or was she merely jealous that Clark would rather steal pleasure from a child, than get it willingly from her?

My mother had tattooed the "what happens in this house stays in this house" rule in her brain, and this was passed down to me somehow. This is why these questions forever remain unanswered. I dare not ask.

This is symbolic though. It shows how much we all condone internalising for so long. If you are filled with so much hurt from happenings in your life and you chose to let it stay in without channelling it out healthily, it hurts you the more. Or how does a house which traps toxicity in heal from it? How do you heal your body on the inside when you don't let the bad things go out?

The story doesn't end here.

Rose's life transitioned to a new life in Dallas Texas, after she was sent out of her mother's house. Here, she was going to live with her father Nick, his new wife, and three other siblings—Cheryl, Mallory and Detrick, who had no business with welcoming her into their home. She remembers the first day she walked in through their door like a bad dream.

"Mom, why is she coming here to live with us?" she could hear the tallest out of all three who she later knew to be Cheryl, ask loudly.

She does realize that I can hear her, right? Thoughts that filled Rose's head.

"She is your sister, and she is coming to live with us for a little while." Nick's wife, Marsha replied.

For Marsha, she had probably been feeling the remorse of entering Nick's life when his marriage was almost ending. The best she could do was welcome Rose into her new house.

"Mallory, Cheryl, Detrick" Marsha called out to her second daughter, and her son. "Come say hello to your sister".

And then, somewhat grudgingly but pretentiously, all three introduced themselves, whilst wearing the most judgemental expression ever, on their faces.

Even though all four kids had bonded later in their life, Rose could not help but feel like an outsider, she wasn't truly their sister after all and the three shared a bond much deeper than she would've ever had with any of them.

Still, Rose and her siblings grew up playing together and experienced growing together like siblings ought to. But Rose wasn't into sober fun. For her, happiness was in the bottom of a bottle—the bottle her mother had introduced her to. So even when things around her were changing, some things still remained the same, like her cravings for alcohol.

Rose soon became a wrecking ball that nothing could ever stop. She was withdrawn from others, especially male strangers. She was filled with so much rage daily. Cheryl, who had managed to get much closer to Rose than the others due to not being self-absorbed like Mallory and Detrick, loved Rose dearly by developed a fear when Rose didn't have things going her way. On a typical day, everything would seem peaceful and perfect, just until Rose gets a random moment where she would fire off and scream at anything and anyone at will. It was like a spell.

There were countless times Nick and Marsha noticed this ruthless behaviour and tried to calm her down to no resolve.

The climax was one night when Nick sat her down in the living room to have a discussion.

"Your drinking, it's got to stop Rose. And this fit of rage, it's hurting everyone around you. It could eventually be the end of you".

Rose flared, "Now you don't get to talk to me about my poor choices" she yelled "Where were you when I made them?"

"Want to play DADDY now?"

"Clark raped me. I was only six. But he did so over and over again yet Momma said nothin 'bout it" the tears that were welled up in her eyes began to flow. "Where was my Daddy then.... hmm?"

She sulked more time as she wiped the snot from her nose with the back of her palm. "All those times I needed you...all those times 'DADDY'" she mimicked. "You were nowhere. And you think you can tell me what to do now?? "

"Send me back to momma"

At Rose's last words, Nick's face lit up in a reaction other than the hurt he was feeling from the reality of her previous statements.

"I can't let you go back their Rose. Things will only get worse" Nick knew that Rose was right, he could have done better. Hurting a child never goes unpunished and now he was seeing the fruits of his actions and inactions. But he could see the future of Rose in Louisville, and it was no good. There was one thing he couldn't do, stop Rose.

Torn to pieces, Nick let his daughter go, again! Or ... what do you do when you see your child about to go through a dark door at this point that they do not want to be saved from?

*****

She was sixteen and back in Louisville after high school. Regressing into a world that had changed so much from what she knew it last to be—a place she no longer felt like she belonged to. Rose left Louisville at the age of 12. Things weren't meant to change that much in four years. But that was the case. Louisville had changed so much that she could barely recognize it.

She said, "The streets look different, the people look different, heck, even the air feels different in my nostrils."

There were the usual side talks from the folks she knew back when she was in town. For some weird reason, they seemed to think that she thought she was better than them because she was coming from Dallas. Rose found it hard to wrap her head around that. All she wanted was to live everyday life. She was not trying to be better than anybody. If only they could look harder, they would see her heart of gold. She never understood why she was often misunderstood. She was still the same outgoing young girl with a bubbly personality, only careful of the people she opened herself up to.

There was Shanna, her friend since childhood. The one person who loved her the most amongst many. My mother, Rose often told me beautiful stories about her friendship with Shanna. They would get on their bikes and ride around town together. Shanna was her escape away from her home life, and as long as they were together, they could survive anything.

On one of their days out in her high school years, Rose and Shanna met Karonce, a cute guy from the Reserved Officer's Training Corps that Rose grew so fond of. Karonce made her feel loved beyond her flaws and outward appearance, for the very first time. He took the time to know her story and gave her all the love and attention she never had. This to Rose, was her own family, in the company of friends who loved her.

They flirted with all the time they had, but sadly before their beautiful love story began, Karonce was enlisted in the military.

This would be the second time Rose's heart was let down by a man. But was confident that if Karonce was meant to be a character in her story, he would one day return to play the part. With this belief, they parted ways. On this night Rose experienced two heart dropping moments because on this same night later when she got home, she discovered that her brother, Uncle Pete, had been shot at when leaving a pool hall. Uncle Pete was down at the local pool hall in and some guys saw him that had previous lost to him in a basketball game. With Pete leaving the next morning going to the Navy, the big shot of the gang Dino felt like "We can't let him leave here with bragging rights." This was a situation it was about what was on him but what is in him you know? With a stroke of luck and fast feet, Pete was able to go out of the back door due to a lady friend telling him that they were planning for him. Pete went out the back door and ran for dear life on foot all the way home where he found Rose crying about Karonce. Upon Rose hearing the news, she didn't hear that she almost lost her brother, but only thinking about that she was losing two men that she loved to the military and would be alone again.

****

She was out of high school— she had stopped along the way, and now searching for ways to get a life for herself—independent of the preying claws of people who had the upper hand. Her first job at Tyco, a chicken plant was just enough to keep her going.

Like a flower that stands out the most in a little garden, Rose made a name for herself. This you could say, earned her the attention she got from both men and women. Rose was notorious for being the life of the party, drinking men under the table, and exploring life in every area imaginable.

She was making solid plans for her life, totally oblivious of the other plans life had for her.

It was a summer weekend, Rose had just concluded her shift for the day and made way to the bus stop nearby to wait for a bus, when she was startled by a familiar voice.

"How much did you miss me?"

For some reason, the voice sounded too familiar, yet she couldn't make out who it was.

Panicking, she reached for her pocket, hoping to find a weapon; a key maybe, a pen, anything at this time would suffice. She finally grabbed a key.

As she turned around to take a strike, she was even more startled. She couldn't believe who was standing before her.

"Ka...Karonce?" she mouthed.

"Are you going to say hello little lady or is that how you greet people now?" the young man let out teasingly.

Rose finally shook herself out of the surprise, "I mean, hello Karonce. What the heck are you doing here? You had me startled "

Karonce moved over and pulled Rose in for a hug. "I can't apologize" he teased with a smile.

"I only thought the first thing to do after serving my military time was to look for you" he released her "...and I'm glad I found you".

Rose let out a shy smile.

Karonce was tall, dark, averagely built and fairly handsome. He wasn't much to look at, but he loved her and that was all that mattered—at the time.

They grew fonder and fonder of each other; hung out playing games, sharing similarities in their bad drinking habit, partying and having a good time. This was the beginning of a relationship that would only stay long enough to see its end.

****

The thing with Karonce ended with toxicity and met its looming end on a night they had both gotten into an argument that revealed Rose's true impression about Karonce's appearance. 'He wasn't much to look at'. That same night, Rose's car had broken down right after their argument. It was at that moment she met Ricardo, this angel of a man who was more than willing to help her fix her car—and her relationship status eventually. Perfect timing! When one door closes, another opens up...right?

Ricardo was slender, hairy, and greasy with a gold tooth in the front of his mouth—typical for a small-town shade tree mechanic. 'Slender, gold tooth'. I bet this reminds you of a familiar character in Rose's story? I thought same. Do you think Ricardo appealing to her because of who he was, or did he remind her of a past character in her life?

You see, oftentimes we don't realize how many times we wind up in a cycle; dating the same people over and over again because unknowingly, we have this affinity to the things or people that hurt us.

"Here's my number if you need my help in fixing your car in near future" Ricardo smiled as he handed Rose a piece of paper that contained some writing, when he was done. "Call me"

And Rose did just that. She called Ricardo to fix everything in her life, except her car!!

The thing is, things hadn't officially ended with Karonce, because, who moves on almost immediately after a breakup argument?

Karonce had been busy with work and had little or no time for Rose. But that didn't seem to matter, she was already hitting thing off with her new guy, laughing and rolling over on the bed, talking for hours. She lied to herself when she thought she could keep it balanced and live a double life with both men, but the receipt of her lie was my brother Arien. My mother, Rose was pregnant with her first child for Ricardo.

I wouldn't say Arien's birth brought my mother and Ricardo together, but I sure know she had to pick a side and she chose him instead. They had more conflicts than they had love. So even though they shared drinking habits that died hard, they got into arguments for cheating on each other, mother suffered abuse, and worse still, they were living in poverty.

Theirs was a symbiotic relationship. Even though there was no love, they needed each other's pockets to survive. And on days like this, my brother Arien served as the glue that held them together.

It was the early hours of noon, and Arien was still in daycare, when Rose began to throw a tantrum.

"Who's she? Huhh" she slammed the TV remote control against the wall. My mother had always been aggressive and assertive. The circumstances surrounding her childhood made her, and it followed her into adulthood. Whenever she was angry, she meant business, and she was that way till she got whatever she wanted.

"What you mean who's she?"

"Don't play me Ric. I know you brought a woman into our home when I left for daycare" she yelled, then groaned.

"Heck, I know you be bringing women whenever I leave Ric."
"I hate you! You've turned out to be just like every other damn man in my life. Good for nothing but hurting women" she let out angrily.

Ricardo, frustrated by Rose's display walked to the kitchen and picked up the bottle of gin sitting on the countertop.

"Gett outta here. Don't be here when I get back!" he said, slamming the door behind him as he walked out.

Ricardo got in his barely functional Chevy and sped off, hoping to find relief in driving, with a bottle of gin by his side.

Angrily as Ricardo left, Rose walked over to the kitchen counter to pour herself a drink—the same that Ricardo had earlier carried. She wondered why she hadn't noticed him before. This infuriated her some more.

Rose broke down into the floor in tears. Her life had become nothing but a living hell full of terrible cycles. She needed something to take the pain away.

Her phone rang continuously beside her, disturbing her from her moment of depression. She wished everyone could just go away, but when she saw the caller was persistent, she was left with no other option.

"WHO THE HELL IS IT?" Rose's rage filled her voice.

"Sheriff Dale of Louisville Police Department ma'am" the voice on the other end responded.

Rose froze.

"There's been an accident on ... involving an eighteen-wheeler vehicle and a Chevy. It was a head-on collision. We've identified one of the victims as your husband..."

Rose didn't wait until she heard more, at that moment she was already breathing hard. More than she was concerned about her husband's state, she thought about her life. The thoughts bombed her mind all at once.

"Where am I going to live now?" "Who's going to love me now?" "What am I supposed to do with a child by myself?" "How will I afford to live here now?" "Do I have face Clark again, and move back in

with my mom?" "Will I be safe? Will My son be safe?" Filled with so much anxiety, she eventually passed out on the floor to escape what was going on with her in her reality.

****

Rose woke up to unusual loud noises in her living room. The first thing that caught her eye when she opened them were figures moving around.

"What... what's going on here" she sprang up from the floor.

Her sight finally settled on one person she identified as Ricardo's sister walking out the door with a photo frame in her hand.

"Gloria" "Why are you taking everything out of our house?" she questioned, confused.

"Our house?" Gloria responded "It became yours when my brother died. So, I take what belongs to me".

Rose was still trying to wrap her head around all that was happening. How long had it been since she got the call from the sheriff and was passed out on the floor? Hours? Days? Weeks? Why was her sister-in-law storming her house to clear stuff.

Her new reality had hit her even more now; she was a widow and a single mother. What was life going to look for her? Would she be reliving the story her mother had lived?

All Rose needed to find was a bottle of Southern Comfort to ease her pain. Day after day and drink after drink, Rose slowly found a happy place to exist, escaping her feelings for a while. It was the beginning of a second chapter. What was this going to be?

****

Karonce waltzed back into her life on a random Tuesday. It was a cool day and Rose, avoiding the many thoughts that plagued her, was at one of her social spots, enjoying the slow music by herself.

"A penny for your thoughts", Karonce said as he crept up behind her. Rose was already smiling before she spun around to find him standing there dressed in all black, with an air of mystery as he smiled at her. He looked taller than she remembered, and he held himself with such grace. She would recognise that voice anywhere and at any time, so turning towards him was impulsive, but she was a little surprised by what she saw. He had a fresh cut, and his cologne took her back to the last time she had seen him. She remembered the lingering hug he gave her, as though he knew that she would leave him just after that.

"You look like you've just seen a ghost", he teased her further when she didn't say anything.

"Well, you could be a ghost for all I know", she chuckled, stepping forward to give him a hug.

"Mm", he breathed, "I've missed you". Rose dipped her head and toyed with her fingers.

"I've missed you too, Karonce. I just had…I needed..I…", she stuttered.

"I was really hurt, but I understand that Airen was in the picture, and you had to do what's best for him", he said.

Rose nodded quickly, still bowing her head. She knew right then that she would welcome his affection without hesitation. Maybe Karonce was just the emotional support that she desperately needed at the time. Or was there something more?

Again, Rose was jolted from her thoughts as little Airen ran into the room, calling, "Mommy, mommy, mommy", in a happy singsong chant.

"Hey little man", Karonce joined Rose in her surprised laughter, picking him up and spinning him till he was dizzy and spent. In that moment, Karonce was distracted from the pain their separation caused him, being taken by Airen. Perhaps this love was enough for him to hold on to and let go of the hurt from the past.

***

Rose and Karonce moved in together, and with Airen, they lived as a functional family. However, their pasts still haunted them. They both needed a way to get past all they'd been through on their personal journeys, and so they both found it—alcohol, the one thing that bonded them more than anything else.

You may wonder what pushes an alcoholic to alcoholism. The thrill of it? Filling a void? Finding love? Escaping reality? Whatever your answers may be, these two found theirs as they downed bottle after bottle. For Karonce, it was his way to escape the nightmares that had become unbearable after his time in the army, while Rose chose the freedom that the alcohol afforded her–clouding the pain from her past. But this was not enough for Rose; not the alcohol, and not even the family dynamic she thought she finally had.

When we go seeking things in life, do we really find what we look for, or do we settle based on what we find available? When I think about my mother's love story, I cannot help but wonder if this was her dilemma. Was she stuck in between the decision of settling with what she had found—Karonce, and continuing her search for what she really wanted? This dilemma would bring her to meet someone new, who would change the course of her life in many many ways— first, by questioning her choice of Karonce.

It was a regular day at Tyco. My mother Rose could not wait for the closing hour. She was exhausted, and returning home to Airen was the only thing on her mind; until she saw a stranger walk in.

He caught her attention, of course. 'Too Tough' was the perfect definition of tall, dark and handsome. His smile lit up the entire room and Rose was left breathless. Time suddenly stood still as she watched him laugh and joke with everyone in the room.

"You must have gotten into trouble too many times with that smile and those eyes of yours, or haven't you?" Rose asked as she found her way to Too Tough, after he had had his fill of cheer with most of the other staff.

"I may or may not mind, especially if you're trying to be the trouble. How about we catch up after work so I can see about this trouble I'm about getting into", was Too Tough's quirky response to my mother's tease that day.

Rose, in that moment, forgot about her fatigue, Karonce didn't matter also, as she was inexplicably drawn to the handsome man before her.

Perhaps, his nickname 'Too Tough', would have served as a warning to Rose, but he had introduced himself as Tommy that day. It was only until later she found out that Too Tough was so called because he was known to rarely ever consider another's feelings besides his, and he didn't exactly like the nickname.

Interestingly, my mother had always had the upper hand in her relationships. Call her a player if you may, but she typically had her way until she met her match and fell in love for real — or so she thought. Like many other relationships, my mother's and Tommy's started with butterflies and flowers, roses and rainbows–all the good stuff; like many relationships, when life showed up, it was easy to see that what they had was not love, only lust.

So, while Rose and Tommy seemed to fall in love with each other some more each day, it did not take long for the other shoe to drop.

"I have something to tell you", Tommy started. Rose smiled. Tommy was finally talking to her. It had taken almost two hours of pleading to get him to explain his sore mood. She reached to his chin and lifted his face, using her index finger.

Whether she was in a bad mood or not, she was happy. Days like this were her escape, visiting Tommy on Friday nights was always the highlight of the week for her—she could relax from the long work week and being a parent for a while. She inched closer as he continued.

"I don't want to lose you, Rose. You're very special to me", he went on. "I was very young and made many decisions based on what everyone else wanted and expected of me. I'm not saying it's right, but I did it".

Tommy went on to tell Rose that he had a very young marriage and was expecting a child soon. Rose already had an idea where the conversation was headed, and it was relief she felt, not fear, having a well-kept secret herself. So, she paused, choosing her words, "There's nothing to be scared about, I always knew. I was waiting for you to tell me." Rose took his hands in hers and squeezed it, reassuring him. She felt closer to him as she told him about her relationship with Karonce, whom she lived with. Too Tough pulled her into a hug before she even finished talking.

"So, there's nothing to worry about?", he asked, obviously relieved. "Absolutely nothing", Rose responded, leaning in for a kiss, more in love than ever. Thus, their affair continued until it all fell apart one day.

****

"Who is this nigga that keeps calling your phone?!" Karonce screamed as he went through Rose's phone. Rose shuddered as she heard his raised voice from the bathroom. Karonce was never angry, at least he knew how to control his temper, especially because of Airen. But nothing prepared him for the heartbreak he felt this evening. He had once again been betrayed by Rose and his anger was explosive. His voice alternated from tiny shrill cries to thunderous cursing. Rose froze.

"I do everything for you! Buy you cars, clothes, drinks, and take care of your kid! Why am I always competing with another man?"

Rose was fearful, but she calmly made her way to him and tried to get Karonce to calm down, but her charm does nothing to placate him this time.

He yelled, "Call him and tell him that you are done with this sneaking around right now!" Karonce had crossed the line. His voice lifted with the wind but thinned much before it in Rose's ears. It was high-pitched gibberish at this point, she did not hear a word Karonce said anymore. Leave Tommy? He was asking her for way too much. So, though she panicked, her hands were shaky, and her heartbeat was loud and intense, she knew she could never choose Karonce over Tommy.

The thought of it alone got her angry, so angry that she impulsively charged at him, screaming, "I hate you! I hate that I ever laid eyes on you! I never wanted you to begin with!"

Karonce and Rose wrestled around in the house as Airen, oblivious to the happenings, sat watching tv in the living room.

"I'll just get my stuff and leave because he's a better man than you could ever be." She shouted as she finally started to get her things together to leave. She was scared as she started to go towards the door, but she knew it was over even before he called out to her,

"This time don't ever come back here!". Rose grabbed Airen and left for her car.

***

"What do I do, what do I do, what do I do?" Rose was frantic as she cried in the car.

"Are you okay, mommy?", Airen lifted his head from his toys he had been fiddling with and asked.

"Yes, baby. I know just what to do".

His voice woke her up, and she pulled herself together and called Tommy. He was calm and soothing as she cried to him, narrating the events that had just happened. Calm and soothing, or cold and removed? There was a bite to his voice—some irritation, maybe—but Rose would only hear it in retrospect, the many times she would replay these words in her head, over and over again, trying to understand them, to make sense of them:

"Rose, I love you. I really do", he pauses, sucking in air in his characteristic way, "But I have a child on the way, and I cannot leave my family to be with you". This was easy for him to say because everyone including if family always condoned his negative behaviours but for once he actually felt bad about hurt someone. A part of Rose died that day. She felt it as she drove about aimlessly for a while. Love had once again betrayed her, leaving her cold, and abandoned. With nowhere else to go, Rose finally settled, with much hesitation, to go to her mother's.

***

"You foolish girl!", her mother thundered at her as she got there. If Rose was expecting a warm welcome and some relief from her troubles, she definitely wasn't getting it.

"You mess everything up!", she continued, "How could you leave a man who takes care of you for a married one? Did he really think he would leave his family for someone like you?!"

Rose could barely hold herself together, but she knew she had to act very fast. Her mother was never a safe haven for her. She was shaky as she asked,

"Can you please take Airen for a while so I can get myself together and figure out what to do?"

Marie was uncaring and displeased, but she grabbed Airen and fixed him some food. Rose left —but she decided to run away altogether, to leave the life and the people she had known to start a new life. She wanted freedom, but where would she go? Who would take her now? All life had offered her was rejection and pain.

As if to answer the questions on her mind, her cousin Rena called her. "Wouldn't you like to come over to Houston for a change?" Rena offered an almost desperate Rose. For some reason, Rose had always trusted Reina. She probably fit into the life Rose hoped to live, being the life of every party and popular for saying, "I may tell you a joke, but I won't tell you a lie". It didn't take much to convince Rose, she needed an escape, she was getting one. But would that be enough for her? Was it the life around her, or the life in her that she was running away from?

I know I said that you are meeting me at a place in my life where I am healing from a lot of trauma, but most people don't realize that trauma can be experienced when you are nothing more than a foetus in your mother's womb. Before I even took my first breath, survival mode had already kicked. All of these stories lead up to this point. When my mother was pregnant with me, she used to live her life as though she was denying my existence – she would still party, drink, hook up with random men while in Houston, and she never bothered to schedule a doctor's appointment the entire nine months that she carried me around on the inside of her. As if that wasn't enough, she equally gave me the gift of her trauma stressors. To be quite honest, I can't help but think that she passed down her scars, her anger, her baggage, and her un-cried tears to me and that is why for the majority of my life I had felt like life was so heavy on me. I was too busy carrying baggage that had nothing to do with me, but it just so happened that curses from my mother's past, and her mother's past caught up to me in my generation too. That's usually how generational curses work— passing down unresolved, unhealed, untouched, and continuing to spread roots for more generations to come. Anyways, back to where the curses started catching up to me in life.

***

It was 1991. My mother was heavily pregnant, and she could have popped at any minute, but she was so tiny that depending on what she wore, you possibly couldn't tell that she was pregnant. My mother was also probably in denial because of the unavoidable question: Who does this child belong to? She had been betrayed way too many times that she could not accept the life that she took part in creating. However, one night, my story almost lost its chance to even begin, and this is why I believe that purpose and God are real. This is because purpose always wins. No matter how hard life tries to knock you down, your purpose will give you life every single time. This night though, it almost didn't. My mother was out in Houston, partying, drinking and having fun with Rena and some of her new friends one night. She was very intoxicated as she was approached by a man, offering her a drink. Though he was a stranger, it was not hard to tell that he found his happiness at the bottom of a Budweiser can, as you can imagine that Rose had too.

The only thing worse than two drunk people in the same room is the said drunk people having terrible tempers, one of them being close to nine months pregnant and hormonal. Though my mother was a woman that was very proud, she was also someone who did not let much bother her. On this night, however, she couldn't help that something overtook her and allowed this stranger to get under her skin. I feel like she had had enough.

"Come here little lady, so I can tell you a secret in your ear." Rose began to breathe very hard as she sat on the man's lap and anticipated his words.

He grabbed Rose and rubbed her leg, while whispering in her ear, "How much for me to show you that you can love me after one night?" Rose, unable to separate the words and her stepfather, in a fit of rage, knocked the man backwards and beat him with a bottle.

She continued to hit him as she screamed and cursed him, "I hate you! I hate you!", till there was blood everywhere. Rena, hearing the commotion, rushed over to take Rose away to the car before the police showed up.

Rena was confused and upset, while Rose sat back, shaking, and crying from fright. Rose thought about how easily she fed into her addictions, allowing men and alcohol to bring her to this terrible yet familiar situation again.

Rena, upset, stopped the car and asked Rose to find her way home. "You ruined my night! You're not welcome back at mine and there's no way in hell I'm leaving here so early to take you home", she concluded.

You can tell that this is a difficult situation—a mix of tempers, addiction, insecurities, being pregnant, with heightened emotions is a terrible combination. Yet, this is where my mother found herself, all leading to her now being homeless, with no one to call. What choices was she left with now? I'm sure calling her mother to apologize was the last thing on her mind but what choices did she have now? So, although she hadn't spoken to her mother, my grandmother, in months, she swallowed her pride, picked up the phone slowly, and called her.

My grandmother was putting Airen to sleep as she picked up the phone.

"Hello, who is this?", she answered.

"I need your help, Mama. Rena left me out on the side of the road, and I don't know where to go ". She went on to ask if she could return home for only a short while. Although at that moment, it felt like the worst, Rose made that call at the perfect time.

On that dark, rainy night, my mother journeyed back from Houston. I envision that I was clueless as to what I was being born into. On the bus, Rose started to panic. She only had a trash bag filled with clothes and wet clothes on. All she wanted was to get home to safety, but she kept thinking, *"I'm going back to being a single parent that came from a broken home full of alcoholics, multiple children, no love, no emotions, all while living with her mother"*, all through the journey back to Arkansas. It became a moment of awakening for her, she was finally coming out of denial. Rose started to rub her stomach as she thought, *"How do I keep my secret safe if I couldn't keep myself safe?"*.

Right there Rose started to have flashbacks of Clark, drunk, vile, and raping her while her mother stood by, doing nothing at all. She remembered crying and begging God to kill Clark. It was the only punishment fitting for a man who robbed her of her innocence and started her on this unending cycle of pain and damage.

"ARKANSAS 10 MINUTES AWAY!", the bus driver screamed,

bringing her back to the present. The bus was slow, but it managed to keep going, amidst the storm. Rose's panicked breathing continued. *"In... out"*, she muttered under her breath, as she tried to focus on her breathing to ease the anxiety that kept her on her toes. Still, she found herself looking at every building and street sign, nervously anticipating their final stop.

Ten minutes flew by, and they were at their destination. As the bus screeched to a halt, the passengers started to push and shove as they made their way off the bus. Rose was anxious, but got off the bus carefully, clutching her stomach, begging for some relief from the pain she then felt more intensely, as she looked for her mother.

Marie was crying when Rose found her. Clark dropped his hands in a show of frustration and said, "I don't know why we came here to get her!", but that didn't matter — not at this moment. Rose never thought she would be so grateful to see her mother. She was grateful that she wasn't really alone, grateful that she had helped with Airen for all these months, grateful that she came out to get her out of her own mess as soon as she called. She fell into her arms as soon as she was close enough. Marie grabbed Rose and held her tightly, crying and whispering in her ears,

"I will keep you safe this time. It's okay. You're okay. Thank you for coming to me."

This was new to Rose. She had never experienced a love connection with her own mother, but she welcomed it fully, needing all the support she could get in that moment. But their moment was short-lived. While

Clark sat and watched them in disgust, Rose suddenly started to struggle to breathe. She winced, clutching her chest and stomach at the same time.

"I need to get to a hospital!", she gasped," A-A-Asthma!".

It dawned on Marie that the streets were emptying out, and they were some of the few persons left at the bus stop. In a quick, panicked swoop, she grabbed Rose's trash bag and nudged Clark as she ordered, "Clark, we need to go!"

The rain seemed to pour out harder, worsening their frantic search for a hospital— the roads were slippery, and it was difficult to see the other cars on the road. Marie tried to keep it cool, but her heart broke with every gasp and grunt that Rose made.

"Help me, Mama. Please!".

Her voice was still pitched, but she was losing strength. Marie could tell. As she turned to try to placate her, she spotted bright red letters that she figured read 'Emergency'. Sweet relief!

Clark drove carelessly into the clinic, hitting several bumps and potholes. Rose knew it was out of spite, but she didn't care. Marie ran into the clinic before Clark could even park the car properly.

She screamed, "Help! We need help! My daughter...she can't breathe, she has asthma!". She barely paused for breath. "NURSE!" "Where are the damn nurses?", she cursed.

Nurse Patricia came in with an air of professionalism. She was quick but calming. She spoke to Rose in a clear, compelling voice.

"Breathe in", she started, "hold it...now, breathe out. Take it easy, focus on breathing." Nurse observed Rose and noticed that she was still clutching her stomach. Nurse Patricia rushed Rose into a room and started checking her vitals.

"How long have you been feeling this way and why are your clothes so wet?", she asked, as she figured that she needed to act fast. Rose was responsive, answering all that she was asked, though she felt little relief.

"Why is she not responding to these exercises? She should feel better if this is just asthma", Nurse Patricia thought to herself as she continued to give Rose the necessary first aid. Soon, she asked her to stand and take a walk, just to see if her breathing had gotten better. She was shocked to see a trail of blood as Rose walked.

"She must be pregnant!", she realized, with renewed concern.

The clinic Nurse Patricia worked at was a rather small one, and she doubted that they could handle the complexities surrounding pregnancy and childbirth, especially not on a dark, stormy night like this.

Still, she made the effort to call the only doctor available, Dr Nweski.

Dr Nweski had little experience in this area, but she knew he had performed the procedure during a home emergency.

"I need to get you a doctor, relax, I'll be back", she calmed Rose before running out in search of him. "I NEED YOUR HELP IT'S

AN EMERGENCY!"

Dr Nweski immediately abandoned his books on hearing those words. He rushed to Rose's room and asked to be left alone with her. The doctor marveled at Rose's size. He looked at her and asked,

"Do your people know you're pregnant?" Rose immediately burst out crying.

"I haven't even accepted that I'm pregnant myself."

The doctor was shocked at her response, but immediately set out to examine her.

"I see the head!" Rose was overwhelmed, nothing could have prepared her for this moment.

She had carried this child for nine months, and because of her great denial, she never had a doctor's appointment or a check-up. Now, reality was catching up with her. The baby was here! The circumstances around my birth were not perfect, but it was a relief that she wasn't alone. That phone call happened at the perfect time.

Now, my birth would mark the beginning of another story, however, one with several familiar scenes. My story! Or should I rather call it, the continuation of some generational history. A famous cycle.

■ ■

CHAPTER 2

NEXT DESTINATION - FIGHT OR FLIGHT

"We are an embodiment of all the things we've seen, the places we've been and the stories of the ones that have gone before us."

As a child, I remember my mother's hesitation to return home to her family and friends. I remember it, but I never understood why. The big cities had always appealed to her, and once she got a taste of such places like Houston, it was too difficult to be satisfied with the small humble Louisville in Arkansas.

Louisville was special in its own way though, with its alleyways and back roads. Some of these roads were so narrow, only one car could come down through them at a time. But the scary part, especially experienced by people of color, was the "sundown law".

You really don't want to be in the wrong part of town at the wrong time of day. There was always a possibility that you wouldn't make it out of that place in one piece.

It could also feel lonely sometimes, with its sparse population and lack of activities. The closest we had to a hangout spot was the grocery store, and the most people I saw at once was in school.

So, I can't say that I don't know why my mother was reluctant to come back. However, for most of my life from a baby to a young child, all I knew was life in Louisville, living with my grandparents. Life with my grandparents was beautiful. I enjoyed seeing them every day, and the warm, cozy life they offered. There was nothing better than waking up on Sunday mornings to the smell of fried biscuits, scrambled eggs, and bacon fresh out of that pan-seared grease. It was aromatherapy to my young nostrils. Looking back on it, it should have been pretty obvious that my grandmother could throw it down in the kitchen—She had what I like to call the "fat gene". She was a short, stout woman with healthy arms, and long, shiny, and slick silver hair that I would've loved to play with if she had let me. The only thing I loved more than her amazing breakfasts was to hear her call out, "Dinner's ready!", in a singsong voice she used for us the children. She really showed out with those home cooked dinners. They would have you in a sleep coma for the rest of the night and part of the next morning too.

Ironically, my mother occasionally gave stern warnings to stay away from my papa and my uncle, Clark jr. My young mind could not understand it, and all I could think about was Papa picking me up, throwing me high in the air and catching me as she said, "Don't go close to them!", her face in a deep frown and panic. She would always raise her crooked index finger as she did so. She never expressly said so, but I could tell that she was uncomfortable with my Aunt Desta too. My mum was only ever completely at peace when it was grandma watching Airen and me. I wanted to tell her that we lived all together in the small house, and it was impossible to avoid them, but maybe I was too young to express myself in this way.

However, it didn't take too long for me to understand. When I think about home, I remember sitting around our old dinner table. It gave a squeak whenever someone bumped into it or moved too close in their chair. My papa would always sit at the head of the table and my grandmother would always sit on the opposite side from him, while all children and grandchildren would fill in the other seats. This was the picture of home for me. This was home for my mother too, regardless of her love-hate relationship with this house and the town. Now, I look back and I remember the exact moment that home became an ordinary house and was no longer the place I found comfort, safety, or any pleasant memories. I realized that my family was far from unified. In one night, my ideal home turned into just a building with halls of horrors. I remember it all vividly.

It was a cold day. My mother was settling back into her life at Arkansas. She was back to working late nights at a convenient store to make sure she could provide for me and Airen now. My mother was thrilled to catch up with her childhood best friend, Shanna who had married Busta, a classmate of theirs.

That day, they sat under the porch and talked.

"Girl, I am only here for a little while. I just hate that I had to come back at all" my mother spoke.

I may have been 3 years old during this time and I was enjoying the cool weather, being out with my mother. She was always busy these days. In my excitement, I ran outside of the shed into this tall man that I remembered used to scare me because he was missing a finger.

"Hello pretty girl and what is your name?"

I retreated to my mother and tried to get her attention about the strange man that had come to the house. My mother, being clueless as to what I was explaining, allowed me to lead her to the front. There, she recognised him, and she immediately went stiff and defensive.

"What are you doing here?" was the hostile greeting that she met the strange man with.

I came to know that this man was one of my mother's many flings in the past. He had heard that my mother had a child shortly after their time together.

"Well looks like nothing has changed with you, but I just came to ask if she is mine", he replied, pointing towards me. My mother was visibly angry.

"No, she's not. Please leave. I don't know why you came here!" The next time I would see this man would be years later in a big truck that he drove.

The man left but my mother remained upset for a long time. She hit me several times, warning me about running out of her reach.

"Now go in the house and take a nap!"

The rest of the day went by slowly till it was time for my mom to go to work. On such nights, my grandmother would watch us. My Aunt Desta would have, but she was mean to us, because she was, in some way, envious of my mother's relationship with my grandmother, and they were usually competitive for her attention. See Desta was a different kind of person and truly her father's child in more was than one in her younger years as well as her older years. Desta, like her sister, had a beautiful smile and was known around town for being the local rebel. Desta stole cigarettes, alcohol, etc basically whatever made her look cool in order for her to feel like she belonged. It brings the question of why didn't home make you feel like you belonged if you broadcast about how you had the greatest parents? Or were you scared to share the deep dark secrets from the house of abuse because people would judge you for where you came from? I recall in my younger years having a love hate relationship with my Aunt Desta only because I really didn't understand her but honestly, I don't think she even understood herself.

That night, my grandmother was fixing us plates of fried catfish fresh out of the pond with French fries as my mother left. Soon, Clark walked up to her,

"Let's go out tonight!", he offered.

He was giddy, having had a few drinks. Marie hated when Clark was drunk, but she did not have the strength for the drama that was likely to happen if she said no. So, she happily accepted to go. She also called out,

"Desta you don't have to watch the kids tonight, you can go out with your little friends if you want to."

Aunt Desta jumped up, and at an instance, was out the door, headed up the road to her friend's house. If it was one thing about

Desta, she was not missing a chance to be in the streets on the prowl. Looking for love in all the wrong places is what they call it right?

My uncle, Clark jr was now the only one at home to watch me and my brother Airen. Airen was gentle and collected, while I was more adventurous. He used to avoid me during play because I could get very rough. Once, when I was two and he was 5 years old, they captured a picture of me pushing him out of a chair. I can still smell the room. It was a cold winter night, the big gas heater was blazing, and we were left in the den of the house, in Clark jr's room. We were watching the TV when he came in and laid down on the floor with us.

"Do y'all want us to play a game?" Clark jr asked cheerily as he held me in his lap, demonstrating the game with my brother.

"It is called tickles", he went on, "and during this game you get to tickle me where I tickle you at".

For many generations, sexually molesting children seemed to be a thing that was passed on to every man in this family. My papa did it to my mom and now, his son's rite of passage was about to start, to create a new generation through us. I panicked when I saw Clark jr start to touch my brother. He made weird noises as he guided his small hands to his private area. But that wasn't all.

"Shh, you will enjoy it soon", he cautioned Airen as he started sobbing quietly.

It was horror I saw on Airen's face as Clark jr suddenly lifted him, flipped him to lie on his belly, and in a flash, took off his shorts. His eyes glazed over as he penetrated my brother, leaving him confused as he continued to lie on his belly.

I had turned to look away, but his "It's your turn now" forced me to face him again. As a 3-year-old child, it was like experiencing a robber come in and take the most valuable gift that you have in the house. I screamed and he tore my young midsection to pieces brutally and unapologetically. I cried and cried. The pain was fierce and unending. Then, in a flash, my mother come in and rushed Clark jr into the heater.

Clark jr was shocked, he hadn't realized that my mother had got off early and was back in the house. He tried to put the flames out on himself, but still, my mother would not let him be. She was enraged. She dragged him in every part of the house and Clark jr tried his best to flee away from her. Neither of them said a word but it was a loud circus — Airen and I would not stop screaming, and everything came crashing down. Soon, my papa, Aunt Desta, and grandmother, hearing the loud noises, started to rush back home.

"Why would you call the police on him? The kids are probably lying on him!" Marie said.

My mother tried to hide her disbelief at the words her mother said to her. She cursed and screamed at her as she changed my clothes. I had started bleeding, and there's no telling if it was my grandmother's words or the sight of the blood that caused my mother's eyes to get blinded with tears in an instant.

"As long as my son is in jail you don't have a mother!", Marie continued, descending on Rose in a frenzied attempt at a fight.

Clark and Desta tried pulling my grandmother and mother away from each other. It was happening all over again. Was it me, Airen or her? Either of us could be switched for the other and we'd have the same result. It was all too familiar. My mother Rose remembered the day I was born and her mother's promise to protect her in the cold stormy night. She wondered where that woman was now, why was Gramma Marie angry at my mother for protecting her own children? Why was someone else always more important than her own daughter? She was never good enough to be saved by her mother.

In this night, too many wounds were created. Was the generational curse broken as Clark jr was reported? My home was never a home after this. There was no love, no warmth, nothing but anger and resentment, forming yet another dark door.

****

Sometimes I wonder how we find ourselves in certain positions—regret, depression, sadness, and self-pity for situations that may not even be your fault. How do we end up with such things as our habits, mindsets, unfortunate events, circles of influence among others? Maybe this is what trauma looks like—I've always had it at the back of my mind that many of the things we pick up in our formative years are not within our control. So, as a child, you may choose to fight rather than run away, and as an adult, you may reject healthy love from others, but these personalities we develop are not decisions made solely by us, but also by influences we have had as children. Such was the reality of Danielle Love's life as it started to unfold.

My mother would often scream, "Be still and stop making all of that noise back there!", in the nights, as we had to sleep in the car. It was 1997, and nights like these were cold and unbearable. We were homeless now, as grandma had thrown us out following the incident of that night. Our daily routine now included finding a safe place to park each night, along with a great dose of fussing and cursing from my mother. We would get up the next morning to wash off in a sink at the washateria, and then head to school, sure to appear like everything was normal.

Airen was 8, while I was 5 years old, and we both knew what anger, disgust and walking on eggshells felt like, because this was all my mother embodied. If it all got too much, she would hit us, and we could never tell what little move her tipping point would be. Maybe this was where I picked my fight or flight response to life, or not. I was the typical child, participating in award assemblies, school programs, being on the A and B honor rolls and getting "Great job on your test Danielle", as a recurring applause from my teachers. Mom also managed to have us look presentable, even though it was never good enough; my long hair went in pigtails, my hand-me-downs were neatly put together, but my shoes were terribly bad — I would wear them until I could feel the wind beneath my feet. Additionally, I was thin, and extremely short for my age. This was the perfect recipe for a good roasting, and I got enough of it daily. I was often greeted with "Cheetah!", and it could be just anyone and everyone in my class. I got this nickname because of the scars that I had everywhere on my arms and legs. It didn't end there. I faced bullying from my family members too. I was called "cry-baby" and referred to as "just a child who knew nothing". These little perceptions followed me everywhere, especially as Louisville was such a small town, with all of our lives intertwining. But little things turn into big things as we grow older, and soon, I started to see myself as they saw me.

I was no longer the sweet girl that got good grades; I became the class clown and the menace in school. It was not my fault, someone else had to take the blame for it, and I was sure to let my teachers know every time they pulled me aside to ask what went wrong. It is one of the things that puzzle me the most, that I would pick up habits and influences from the people around me, blame the same people but these little offences were only seen as my wrong, nothing about the situations that made me become the way I had become. I also thought, isn't life easier when we only see it from one point of view? This informs what is right and what is wrong to these people. So, my "tainted" perspective of life was formed as a result of being a victim in and out of school. Life was always happening to me and there would always be someone to take the blame.

Fall festival was coming up and I was excited about our class party. Usually, every child was assigned something to bring to school to help with the party. My excitement died soon enough, as we couldn't afford to get anything.

"Danielle, go to the office now! I have had enough of your disruptions today!" Mrs Wardoff was visibly upset.

This was the fourth time in three days that she would be sending me out to the office for misconduct. Mrs Wardoff didn't know that I was only avoiding the question she had asked earlier. On days like this, I was happy to leave the classroom for a bit, because it meant that my mother would be called, and I would be sent home. But that wasn't the case today. Mrs. Jean, the school counselor, decided she wanted to have a talk with me instead. I rolled my eyes at the mention of this. I really just wanted to leave. I wanted her to call my mom so we could get over and done with it already.

"Well, since you don't want to come into my office, how about I sit here and talk to you. What's going on with you? You went from being so full of love and laughter to being upset all the time. With a middle name like Love, I would think you are the sweetest person ever, and I know she's in there somewhere", Mrs Jean continued in her low-toned voice.

It is true that I wanted to leave, but something about her words made me soften a little. She remembered my name. She wasn't yelling at me. So, when she asked me to get up and take a walk around the hallways with her, I agreed.

"Is everything okay at home?" I didn't hear much of what Mrs Jean had said, I completely zoned out to avoid her questions, but this one stabbed right at me.

Home. It was non-existent to me. All I remembered was my mother's recurrent words, *"What happens at home stays at home. They don't care about you, I do."* I remained silent, and poor Mrs. Jean concluded that since I was calm enough, I could return to the party going on in my class.

I was about to step into the classroom when Mrs. Wardoff firmly asked again,

"Where are the chips that were assigned to you, Danielle?"

I panicked all over again and ran out of the classroom. It felt like an attack. It felt like she knew my secret life at home. It is amazing how the slightest words at times can trigger us. As I think about it, a lot of my issues with other people wasn't what they said, but what I was thinking about, and the things I was dealing with at that time. And this is the case for many of us. You would laugh if I called you a stick, because you know you are not a stick. If you have body image issues, however, that could trigger something terrible in you. It's the same way we know at times that were not ugly, worthless, stupid, or unstable, but we would typically internalize it if it was thrown at us in the times we deal or have had to deal with issues so related.

As I ran out of the classroom, I hit everything in my way. I was screaming, as tears streamed down my face tearing everything along the way, I think this may have been me experiencing PTSD symptoms for the first time and no one knew not even me. WHY WOULD SHE PICK ON ME LIKE THAT?! I continued to run blindly in the hallway and only stopped when I heard a gentle voice behind me. It was Mrs.

Jean again. She asked,

"Danielle what's going on with you, did you not bring the things from home like you were asked?"

I cried as I finally told Mrs. Jean that I didn't bring anything from home, because my mom didn't get me stuff that we couldn't afford. She continued to ask questions about my life at home. For the first time, I thought it was safe to tell someone that my life didn't look like the lives of the other children. I was angry and continued to cry as Mrs. Jean sat beside me. She patted my hair gently and went on, "What are you eating every day?" "Can your mom afford to feed you most days?" "Are you being hit when mommy becomes upset?" I answered everything truthfully. I had come to trust Mrs Jean and I thought she was going to be the help we so desperately needed.

What I learned that day is that help hurts. I understood why my mother insisted that what happened at home should stay at home. I see this situation in many ways as an adult, but as a child, I only thought that I was getting what I needed in that time. I told the truth to get help, for me and my family, but it seems like it all started to go downhill from there.

"Hi Danielle, I am Mrs. Johnson, how are you doing today?" This older woman came into the room, looking all serious and professional. She had a kind smile, but a part of me that knew something was wrong.

"I just want you to know that you are not in trouble, we just need some additional information from you." Mrs. Johnson went kn.

She asked a lot of questions, and honestly, part of me was equally relieved that I no longer had to act like I was okay, I didn't have to be angry about anything anymore. After answering questions for what could have been two hours, Mrs. Jean said she was going to call my mom. She asked me to stay after school with her, and help her with a project. I didn't mind, so I found a pencil and a piece of paper and set to do some drawing. I sat there and got lost in the art, not realizing how much time had actually passed. When I finished, I went to look around in the hallway, and found that everyone had left. Everyone except me. I roamed a little in the hallways and started to hear some voices from Mrs. Brenda's office. She was the school secretary. I recognized her voice and that of Mrs. Jean.

"Do you know how easy it is to overlook issues like this? It's easy to think the child is only seeking attention", Mrs Jean was nor as soft spoken as Mrs Brenda, but I heard the compassion in her voice and my throat was suddenly tight.

"I hope everything gets better for her", Mrs Brenda made a move that made her chair squeak. I ran as fast as I could, back to my drawing in her office.

It was hard to pretend that I had not overheard a bit of their conversation, but I didn't have to pretend for too long.

"You'll be going home with your father for a short while. Your mum will come to see you as soon as she can".

These were the last things I heard Mrs Brenda say that day, as the man I barely knew stood, towering over both of us, stretching his hand towards me, and smiling a weird, crooked smile.

(My mom and dad always had a complicated relationship because he lived a double life. He wanted her to accept being the other woman and when she didn't, I always got the short end of it. I remember calling him several times as a kid when my mom would get in these rages, begging him to come get me, and he would either not answer, or pretend that I had the wrong number. I grew to find that it was his number all along. The first time I remember meeting him was when I was about five years old. Me and my brother Airen used to go to his hometown, Crystal Springs, AR, with him. It was years later before I would go back down there with him to live due to being court ordered by a judge at age 16. One of my favorite memories is when I got to hold my baby brother Peter for the first time, and I became a big sister. The only thing I wanted to do was hold him and play with him all day. Back then, I actually really liked my dad's baby momma Martle. I think between my dad having inappropriate conversations with my mom, my mom bringing him food, and Airen coming along even though he isn't my dads's son, the baby momma began to frown on the fact that I even existed. Till my mother completely stopped letting me go up there—it was because the woman, my stepmother, had become abusive to us. She never whooped her own kids, but me and my older brother on my dad's side Trey always caught it. When my dad would leave for work, we never knew what kind of horror we had planned for us that day. She treated us like maids rather than kids. On some days, she would ask us to jump on one leg, just to punish us. She and her sisters would

sit around and laugh as we struggled, and if we stopped, we got beat with extension cords. I wondered if my dad knew and didn't say anything or if he didn't know. One night, he sat right there and watched as she beat me up for something that never happened. He sat casually and didn't say a word. I got all the answer I needed. IT IS CRAZY HOW MUCH WE PAY FOR THE SINS OF OUR PARENTS!)

As my father stood before me that day in school, the only thing I wanted in that moment, was the familiarity of my mother's rickety car, her shaky voice and Airen, holding me to sleep as she screamed about one thing or another.

She did much more than that. She started with screaming down the walls at school. She screamed at me, at Airen, at random people who stared, pedestrians who were slow, everyone. The day ended with my mother beating me endlessly. She did not stop when I screamed and cried and begged. Airen joined me in crying and begging, but it didn't change much. She was livid, and all I remember is the constant, "Do you want them to take you from me?" It resounded too many times in my head, and it shut me up, because I was only trying to find us help. For the first of many times to come, I felt voiceless and helpless.

At this age—eleven, I saw myself getting into more and more fights at school whilst trying to form an identity. I would often get into fights with people because, I told everything. It became gossiping, something I did to take away from what I was feeling.

During this time, my brother Airen was fast becoming the ladies' man and was sexually active. I remember the many times he had to run away from brothers who were angry about Airen's interest in their sisters. I always ran away with him. But then because he couldn't fight with his size and height, I became his punching bag too. At the age of 14, he was 5'9 and 164 solid.

We house hopped a lot. From homes, to apartments, to being back in the car, to homeless shelters especially when my mums went to college while getting her associates. It wasn't too long after she graduated before mum found us a place to live in. She had started to work two jobs — as a cashier and as a cleaning lady, and we were put on government assistance. *You know despite what we went through with her I saw her do everything but quit even when she went to jail for writing hot checks in order to get us school clothes. That during a time where we had to go back to living with my grandmother and Clark where Clark always picked on me to make feel less than but surprisingly, I don't have a lot of memories from this time. Trauma has a way of sealing itself until you open the door, right?* On most days, while she was at work, we would go over to our Auntie Shanna and Uncle Busta's house. Here, Airen and I would often get in trouble for fighting each other. We were so young, but we had such high energies. To keep me from being so aggressive towards Airen, and to dispel some of this energy, my mother thought it was a good idea to have me join a sports team. I played basketball. I came to enjoy it a lot. One day, I got terribly hurt. It was a normal practice day until it got really rough with this girl. We both struggled for a bit and things became intense. In a flash, she had pushed me to the latch of a door and I started bleeding. There was a gash in my head, and I remember seeing blood everywhere. I still have the scar to this day. I was scared and assumed that I would be sent to the hospital, but that never happened. I was only given liquid stitches. That event, as I advanced in years had me wondering about my purpose in life. I was definitely meant to be something great, seeing that I have been through several life-threatening situations and still made it out alive. From landing on my back when I fell from a massive magnolia tree, to wrecking down 100ft drop off after prom, to the many times Airen would hurt me and get away with it. One I remember clearly, maybe because I also still have that scar to this day, is of one night when Airen and I had both been playing. It was in grandpa's house (I had loved it there. He was literally my favourite person; he made me feel safe and spoiled me silly. Maybe it was his way of making up for all the times he could not be there for my mum. He gave me the one picture I had of a happy family, with food, laughter, and prayer. But then he passed, and I never experienced family in this way anymore.) That night, I decided to get on the treadmill to show Airen that I was faster. We were both runners with good speed in our school athletic teams. So, Airen took the challenge, and we got running.

"I won! I won!", I was too happy to scream as I neat Airen's speed. "Sore loser!", I teased as I saw his face drop.

Airen wasn't having it. He pushed me with so much force and anger that I fell and got a burn. I don't know what surprised me more, Airen's violence or my mother's outburst.

My mother ran into the room yelling so angrily, "You should have sat quietly in a place! Why are you always so restless?!"

My response was weak, but it was loud enough, "It was Airen who pushed me, why are you shouting at me? You never say anything to him", I sulked.

Maybe I should have kept quiet, because the person I saw after I spoke was unrecognisable. She was angry at something bigger her than me. This wasn't about anything that happened that night, it was simply an animal attacking its prey. I often wondered where this deep rage came from. Did I remind her too much of herself when I acted a certain way? I ran to my grandpa for comfort. He held me gently, put me in his bed, and tried to make mother calm down, but he couldn't bring her out of her rage. He did keep me away from her until she calmed down.

Interestingly, I got my first period on this day. I'm now sure that it was my body's response to being so stressed. Earlier that day, I was alone with him. He had the cast from the previous night when I had pushed him off the top of the bunk bed. It was one of our rough-play moments. It was a cool afternoon and for some reason, I was happy. I sat down to watch a tape, but Airen grabbed the remote control before I could get it.

"Give it back!", I screamed.

"No". Airen was known for his defiant one-liners.

I got very angry as we continued to argue over what to watch, and in a fit of rage, I threw a VCR tape at him. It was one of my mom's favorite movies, and though we hid the tape quickly, Airen told her everything that happened while I was in the tub, just to get back at me.

I was oblivious to my mother's rage. I was taking a bath and singing like I had no care in the world when I suddenly started to gag hit with a belt from behind. I was terrified. I struggled to get out of the tub and pleaded with her to stop. She didn't. She continued to hit me in a blind rage, using her hands when the belt failed. I begged to go pee and locked myself in the bathroom. I imagine what happened next from my mother's perspective and I cannot bring myself to understand how inhumane she could be towards her own child. I sat in the bathroom, planning an escape, only to find blood trickling down my legs. I screamed. It was the loudest I could go. I was terrified and confused. When my mum came to the bathroom, she continued from where she had stopped, and only gave me what I need for my menstrual flow after she had beaten me to her satisfaction.

As sad as it was, that wasn't my saddest day. I'll never forget the day that my grandfather passed. I learnt grief and loss at an early age, but I was in mid-20's before I recognized I had truly never grieved. I had experienced quite a lot beforehand — a loss of safety, a loss of trust, a loss of love—but I was about to get my first dose of grief at an early age. We were driving to Dallas because they had called us all in, telling us that grandfather had a limited time. I remember that we went in there to find him so childlike. He lay in bed, all smiles and laughs, but he could not recognize anyone except me. I sat beside him, surrounded by everyone else, not really knowing what was about to happen. The house we typically went to for laughs was in that moment, filled with sadness and gloom.

My grandfather died with his characteristic smile on his face and to this day, that is how I see him, and no one could ever change it, whatever bad I may hear about him. I refused to attend the funeral. I don't know if it was because I really didn't feel good or secretly, I didn't know how to deal with losing him. I felt unprotected and alone again my terrorizing thought was "Who would protect me from my mom now?".

My mom got very depressed after his passing. And in this entire process, I lost my childhood. Another huge loss for me. I couldn't live like a child anymore, no play, no leisure. I had to become my mom's caregiver, maid and comfort. I could only sleep in her bed; I wasn't allowed to sleep in mine anymore. At first, it seemed like it was all for her comfort, but soon, it was the best thing, as my brother started to act out on me sexually. On most days, I could only stay in the house to cook and clean or go empty my mom's 'bedside pot', as she found that simply couldn't bring herself to leave the bed and go to the bathroom on most days, while my brother was allowed to go anywhere and do everything.

I had begun to learn uncanny things from my parents and their families. Of course, it was inevitable. How to give, receive and express love in the most unhealthy ways, how to discipline people with aggression whenever they did something wrong, uncontrolled rage and impulsively hitting people to communicate you've went too far, alcoholism and drinking through problems, manipulation, how being messy and gossiping was cool as long as it was not my business to keep people's attention, how titles enable disrespect and abuse, how to manipulate religious views into making people do what wanted (the religious trauma that came from that would be the start of a completely different book, God gave us free will but as human we force each other to choose according to our values?) toxic relationships with no boundaries, pride and being stubborn, not knowing how to apologize, how being affectionate makes you weak, being self-centered, and cheating (this, I know I got from my dad because hands down he was the only person I know that talked to 20 women and lived at home with his baby momma with no drama with the other women. I used to strive to be like him and actually became him when I was younger between ages 18-24 but eventually, I grew out of it). Now that I think about it, it occurs to me how people pick on generational traumas and scars and carry it on through their lives, most times unconsciously. The events in my family were not okay but had taken place across generations so much that it felt normal. As a domino effect, or led my mother, grandmother and even Airen and myself make decisions that were not right. The abuse was only a part of it. Our lives —Airen's and mine—began to unfold in a strangely familiar way. But then, my mind is often reinforced by these popular words from my late grandfather; "it's not about where you start at, but where you finished."

CHAPTER 3

A PROBLEM, OR 'THE PROBLEM'?

"You can't always control the storyline or the narrative, but you can always control the character."

I have, through my journey, come to realize that oftentimes when our lives are rocky, we expend effort trying to figure out what the problem is. Hardly do we ever pause to wonder, if we are our own problems, or if we perhaps, have had a role to play in aggravating or alleviating the situation. It is easy to look outward than it is inward because you can't do the work for another person right?

I do not say this as a license to be hard on oneself--*it would be rather unfair to beat yourself up about the things you go through, or drown yourself in taking all the blame*—rather, this goes to mean that no matter what we go through in life, we have the responsibility of participating in rescuing ourselves from the situation in question. Sometimes, we spend so much time complaining about the problem and don't even realize we are giving ammunition to the problem, and that the people we tell them to do not even realize that it is only hurting us. We want these people to feel sorry for us, when we could use the time, we spent sulking and expecting a savior, to find the solution ourselves. *Example: That toxic relationship that you want to work so bad but you chose not to recognize it's a sinking ship with no life rafters.* But why? What about this familiarity do you need to serve you at this point? Do you realize that you can miss the memories with someone and not miss them at all? With all these questions I want to give you a gift that was given to me by my amazing therapist. During one of our sessions, one of the most monumental aha moments that I experienced was my therapist once asking me was "Do you realize that you can like parts of a person and not like that person at all?".

The truth is, it is so much easier to remain in the place where you are. The thought of seeking a change and fighting for it, may at the place you stand, seem infeasible, but instead of moving on at this frequency, you should learn how to redirect your path. My story has shown me that as humans, we would rather deal with what feels comfortable and familiar, than exploring a new path of healing and letting go because we simply will do anything to avoid emotional pain.

This is why it often feels like we've moved on, but in reality, we are only moving on with the same old baggage to a new place. Then, we relive the same cycles and begin to wonder why things aren't changing.

The ignorance of these realities was my life in my teenage years well into adulthood especially in romantic relationships. My high school years were full of juvenile delinquencies and by this time I had been court order by a judge to move to Crystal Springs, AR with my dad. Before being court ordered to go to my dad's, I had been in juvenile 3 times and was warned the last time if I came back, I would be there until I was 18. During these years, I learned a lot from the jailers that were at the juveniles and even what it was like to be in a locked down facility. "Jones, you got that attitude in your pocket today?" would normally be how the guards would determine how the day would go with me. I remember one night I got so bad the Warden, Tina, came to talk to me and asked why I was so angry and back then I really didn't realize I was simply fighting to prove that I was enough and worthy. A mother putting her child in a cell just to spend a child support check in peace isn't exactly the warm invitation to love and peace. I had let my background shape my character so much that even though I had been incredibly talented, I was a terrorist in a way of speaking. From the time I got out of juvenile and now in Crystal Springs, Ar I was now fighting for my mothers and my father's attention that "I'm not okay." In my 9th- 11th grade years, I would have fights with other people just because I knew that was the only time I would see my dad, to embarrass people with jokes, be a bully because of my size, and had an attitude that could bend a room. On a given day I would be funny, or I would be mean but there was no in between. I was drawn to alcoholism more than ever, threw the dopiest party in the school cafeteria and had gotten in several drunken fights with being around people that shared the same intimate relationship with pain as I did. These, for me, were epic nights. In high school senior year, you couldn't miss more than twenty days in order to graduate, and I think I was suspended every other week or in ISS for something. There were school counsellors like Mrs. Judy and my favorite teacher Mrs. Cadance, who kept an eye on me to make sure I stayed on my coursework and wasn't getting into trouble every other day. No, matter how much negative I showed these two women they always had an higher expectation out of me.

For everyone else though, it would be fair to say that it was expected for me to show out an often the highlight of the school day. My life on the outside was a mess; it was filled with days of my brother Trey and I looking for a place to stay after school as we were now totally abandoned. Our father had moved with his baby mother and three kids to another part of town in Crystal Spring with only school to depend on for our essential needs. At the age of 16, I remember having to sleep in the playground every night and having to wake up from there to school in the mornings. While I was in class cracking jokes, being flirtatious, and writing poetry, nobody really knew that I was self-destructing on the inside. It became a call to establish relationships just so I could find a place to lay my head every night. It was a battle my brother and I had to fight together, yet separately. While I handled things in my own way, Trey had people draw to him because he turned his pain into humor or defiance. I remember countless of times (what I now know as dissociation) him conjuring stories about other people just to have some attention from somebody because what attention did, he have outside of negative behaviour? He had a fan of people that enjoyed only one thing about him, a good laugh because on a given day, he was notorious for showing out. Me on the other hand I struggled to let anybody close to me or to allow love from anyone.

Everyone always says that your first best friend is typically your siblings or cousins but that was far from true because my first best friend was a stranger to me. The first person that ever genuinely took me in was Jerry, and even though my relatives lived literally five minutes away (the town was really small), they never cared to check on me, not for once. I remember when he first found out that I was homeless he snuck me into his room through a quiet house and gave me chili dogs to eat. I am sure that's why I am a grade A lover of chili dogs, so you see not all trauma responses are bad. Jerry's grandparents were elderly, his mother was deceased, and his father was currently in jail, so Jerry typically did what he wanted to. I remember days where we would just roam the streets in whatever clothes we could find that matched, get high, eat, and talk about life. As kid life was cars, money, and girls even back then I had a knack for hearing problems and consoling people.

Whenever I think about it, I could say that I didn't have family from either side to know whether I was dead or alive from day to day. Well, besides the cousins that I saw at school; Kihma, Vick and Faith. On days when Vick wasn't being egoistic because he was a star football player, these three in their little way, looked after me as much as they could as kids. Vick's talent gave him fame, and it was all people saw--*not who he was or what he struggled with*. His popularity had given him so much immunity to things; I remember that on one particular day, he beat Kihma up. Kihma had addressed Vick as the 'town whore' to her best friend, who also happened to be Vick's girlfriend. I cannot tell fully what had transpired that day, but Vick was so mad. After the fight, no one had said a word to Vick about his unruly behavior that day. He was that revered. It wasn't until my senior year when the abandoned house I was living in was burned that that I got a chance to see more sides of Vick. No one is perfect but it was then that I recognized that he's not a bad person he just had ways that I didn't agree with at times because he had a good heart outside of his athletic popularity.

I think this popularity was beneficial to me. I gained from it especially on days Vick stood up for me. It allowed him to do so with ease. I can recall once that I had gotten into a fight with a girl at school that I was devoted to showing out, even with a cast on. I had pulled her pants down and bullied her in front of everyone and as soon as the bell rang the show began. "Why did you pull my pants down!" she screamed and clapped her hands multiple times and, in that moment, I could see it was a fight that was about to happen. I blacked out throughout the fight, and I only remember being pulled off of her with others explaining what had happened. The fight got dirty when her cousin Demarcus jumped into the fight to defend her. That day, Vick came to my rescue. He flew through the crowd to get him and the football team grabbing at him because this was a Friday night lights day. I screamed in the principal's office in panic "I didn't want to fight her!" as everyone looked around because that may have been the first time, I didn't brag about fighting with an arrogant attitude. What no one knew was I had just had a meeting with the school officials stating that I continued to get in trouble that I wouldn't graduate or be able to go to prom. While everyone may have thought that I didn't care about anything, these two things secretly meant a lot to me.

My other cousin, Kihma was a character in her own world. Kihma was an extremely smart young woman, only, she was always caught up in people's drama a lot which was inherited because her mother, Aunt Samantha was the same way. I believed it would be her undoing honestly because it was as she lived in everyone else's drama to escape the drama of her own personal life. She was athletic as well and skilled in several of areas but her loyalty to others was not her best practice. Faith, on the other hand was the 'old faithful of the town' but despite her start in life she came out to be the greatest mom and wife that I know later in her life. She was the life of the party and full of laughter. We loved her no less though but equally I don't think we understood what she mentally went through and used sex as coping skill. I could call these three my childhood supporters where we all struggled with things, we all coped the best ways that we knew how to even with each other. I do not believe that we shared the same reality, but I would say there were similarities. Each one of us—all three, were on a quest to discover ways to cope with ours.

Outside of these 4 there was a stranger that entered my life by chance from a birthday party invitation that became a constant for the rest of my life. Brina was the person that everyone loved in school and those that she encountered for her beauty, intelligence, and just simply being herself. When I met Brina for the first time, I thought she was weird but as time went on, I realized she was unique with a love that I needed at the time. Where there is great love during this time came great misfortune in my eyes. Anything that came with love equally had to come with chaos and pain or so I thought. Brina was loving and came from a loving family but also a strict religious family as well. The plan was to only be friends with Brina but that turned in to a romantic relationship along the way and that became a novel within itself. Brina looked out for me, encouraged me, and saw or heard things about me that no one else knew kind of like a human diary actually. Her reward for that was pain and suffering that came from her family because who she chose to love. Her mother Teresa hated the idea of Brina loving me and in these days, it was "that's still your mother" that justified several of abusive nights rather it be physically, mentally, or emotional. Through all of this and even through my hellish way, Brina still found a way to find a light in me no matter what happened. I vaguely remember one day during my senior year of high school walking down the hallway and being pulled into a classroom. "I don't want you to be scared when you get called to the office, but Teresa is up there with the police to take you to jail. "What was happening was Teresa preparing to press charges on me for statutory rape on her child because I was 18 and she was 16. The saving grace that day (even in your foolish times God has a way of intervening on your behalf) the law had just past that gives persons 16 years of age the right to consent. In 5 years, Brina and I had never been alone together to do anything due to constantly being monitored but this was Teresa's way of ensuring that her family could no longer receive any embarrassment. There was several days after that for the next 5 to 15 years that every chance that Teresa got, she made her feel bad because of who she chose to love in her teenager years and well into her adulthood. Religious trauma is something that is commonly experienced but rarely spoken on because you know that doing the Lord work huh? Throughout every story of my life, regards of the storyline Brina has always played a part in some capacity.

Living with Larry was not seamless or did not make my life easy. It only made things a little less difficult. There was still that struggle with trying to survive. I was high every other day. For me, this was an escape and more extensively, a strategy for survival. Here's what it looked like; every night, Larry would sneak me some food from his home and would wait until it was really late so that he could successfully sneak me into his house without having to answer any questions from his grandmother with whom he lived. Things continued in this pattern, but not for long.

It doesn't take a lot of time for an elderly person to sniff out something fishy when there is. Larry's grandmother soon discovered me, and eventually attempted to put me on food stamps while I was at school. That day, DHS got called. I remember it like I do my name, because it would eventually become the first time any of my family members would show up in my life after a long while and my second round of official business at school.

****

I walked into the principal's office that day to see two adults who I recognised as my father and his sister, Aunt Tanya being interviewed by a couple of DHS officials. I was hit by a rush of emotions, why were they here when in reality they really didn't care? I was young, with nowhere to go and no one to look after me. If there was nothing else, I understood at that age, I for sure understood that children my age needed family but as I got older understand family is everything. I mean a had version of a family, but why did they choose to be absent instead? The officials invited me to take a seat and began to ask me a couple of questions, most of it relating to my father who was seated in the same room.

"This man is not a parent. He does not take care of me" I remember this line as my only suitable response to all they had to say. I was fearful in that moment with saying it seeing as how the first time I told him that's how I felt he picked me up by my neck with one hand in anger. My father's sister Tanya chided me with her eyes, she rebuked me, scolded, ranted. But I did not care the slightest bit. I was hurt, broken and disappointed so in that moment I wanted them to share the same fear as me. I had a response for her too, and I did not hesitate to scream it aloud. "Y'all are here only to save your skin!" My shrieking voice echoed in the whole room. Never have I stood up to my aunt the way I did that day, but it was liberating. It was the beginning of something I could never see coming, learning how to advocate for myself.

My life advanced from there to an abandoned house where I was again, left to take care of myself. How does one define 'terrible,' or even quantify it? Whatever your response may be is exactly what that house had been. I can re-picture the piss holes on the floor, roaches running everywhere from corners to walls and all over the floors. The rats! The climax of my nightmare. Still, I lived this nightmare every night with no one, and no one's care. This house smelled every day and was barely still standing at this point before it was burned down. There were several of days the only way what I got by at night would be to talk on the phone with Brina and cry until I went to sleep or laugh with her about school stuff.

You see, the most important thing about living with life's ugliest sides is in learning to survive, to thrive. Through my years, I have come to learn that when life gives you the worst, you wield healthy tools for yourself—tools to help you survive through it all. This realisation has become my cheat sheet to whatever issues I face in life. I have seen how well it works. At this stage of my life, my tools for escape became poetry and art. When I was in class, I could get lost in a good piece of drawing or poetry for a valuable period of time. I would get fully immersed, enough to forget that I had any troubles, or that I even belonged to a world where troubles existed.

The opening quote in this chapter tells of one thing, finding your character and being it despite how nasty or devastating the plot is. I think this is widely metaphorical to my story, I'll tell you how so.

Writing short stories gave me the chance to rewrite mine. In my stories and poems, I lived the life I always dreamed of, had the kind of love I wanted to have and did all the things I wanted to do. This was where expressed exactly what I felt and knew exactly how to say it. It was the literal definition of using the pencil to create my own narrative, my own story. I always had the tool, I didn't just know when to use it, until it was alone time. It was then that I found my identity and developed my character by creating another character.

Dearest Love,

As the seasons change and birth ages into death dearest love my friend and foe, I see you still remain close,

In the heart of a mother to a child or from soul to a soul tying all of those that have you close to twists and turns in fate,

In all these years of seeing you and knowing you dearest friend and foe you have been the smile through tears and one's greatest fear,

What makes you so wanted but so painful to have near and dear creating wars, pain, and darkness,

Or rather could it be that I need to see you through a different pair of windows to change the vision of you in my soul,

To have you close in the warmness of the spring instead of feeling you in the coldest of winters,

Stay away stay out don't come close you bring destruction when I open the door to allow you in dearest friend,

I need you to be a friend but rather you have proven yourself to be foe time and time again,

Raging storms, war, terror that throws off the course of my steps going backwards instead of forwards why do you haunt me as you do,

As I look back you may be foe now but once upon a time, we were friends too,

Take me back to that 90s feeling when we talked and laughed about how good it felt to be your friend dearest love,

As I look forward towards the dark hallway I sit and dwell in I remember that some friendships must come to an end.

Sincerely,
Your Secret Admire

I've learned to see everything that happens to me in life, in both a good and bad light. I believe that all the things you've had to endure helps you to understand yourself as a person on a deeper level from trial and error. From here, you learn your capabilities, strengths, boundaries, interests, dislikes, and much more. Sometimes, we never feel comfortable enough to be ourselves within society, so we conform to the identity and expectations that they have for us, or adapt so much to the situations around our life that we change with it. Yes, when we do this, we lose and forget who we are, and we may go our whole life and never find that person again. It is important that you find yourself and keep you. I call this *'participating in your rescue'*.

Finding my identity, and my voice again was like breaking through a door and not caring how people saw what came out of it on the other side. It was freedom, but as you know, freedom comes with a price. For me, freedom came with the cost of being different and rejected because I no longer wanted to camouflage with everybody else. Freedom came with saying goodbye to people that I still love till, this day, but can only do so from a distance. Freedom came with change that scared me, angered me, but freed me in the end.

Back to the storyline, I was getting ready to graduate high school during this time period after several threats of "if you just show up and be quiet, you'll graduate." from several of my teachers. I was still doing my normal young, wild, and free habits I just got better at being manipulative which would be a blessing and a curse in the next chapter of my life. One of my worst memories of my senior year was our house, that I alone was now abandoned at, burned down with all of my senior stuff in it. I remember that period of time was chaos, and no one really knew that my mom wouldn't even send money from my child support check that she was getting with me not being there to help get me clothes. I remember having to wear used underclothes, too big clothes, everything to survive that year. A great period again in my life where I experienced great loss.

CHAPTER 4

PICKING UP THE TORCH

"Sitting in a dark place requires no work. Reaching for the doorknob opens you to all the work there is, hiding behind that door."

The only way to ever truly move is forward, but sometimes, when you are coming from a dark place that you had been in for so long, adapting to the light takes a long process. At the time, this analogy summed up my life. My journey had moved from high school to college where I was figuring myself out, learning new things, and thriving. During this transition from high school and college I was just in a relationship just simply to have a place to live and hadn't even begun to start figuring out of what adulthood was. Most people are excited about high school graduation but for me it was a nightmare. The night before my high school graduation my Uncle Martin, who took me in after our house burned down, sat me down and said, "You know the night that you graduate you gone have to find you someone to be that night and every night after." Being 18 years old and not having a role model I immediately went into panic mode because was I really about to go back to living on the streets or out of a car? Graduation night I couldn't even enjoy because I didn't know what life was about to bring me. In a weird way college saved my life despite that chaos that took place to get me there I had arrived. Learning people and learning the place I had a chance to reinvent myself and so I thought I had. But you see the truth is, I was still the Danielle

Love Jones. The one that had been shaped by hurt and desperation for survival. The fight for my life, the fight to be seen, loved, and heard, had continued to make me physically aggressive even in college. There were times when I knocked someone out their shoe in a party, beat someone up from one end of an apartment building to the other end during a kickback I threw, and picked someone up twice; the first time, I threw this person through a door. On the second, it was in a field. All in the name of respect because this is what respect had been modelled to me to look like, fear.

For the most part of freshman year, I thrived in learning; people, places, new things, but it became even harder as I advanced. I was wildly notorious, I would say. Notorious enough to possibly earn a spot in the stories of my schoolmates to their children from epic nights of house parties. The entire struggle to survive had put me in a lot of toxic situations and bad relationships that I would have probably never found myself in; the need to belong had put myself in sorority that made things even harder for me. I didn't realize it then, but as I think about it now, I had subjected myself to getting hit, or abused just so I could maintain a place to fit in, a family if you will. I recall throughout the sorority process several of nights where I struggled with things that happened simply because my thoughts were "When am I ever going to get a different version of family that doesn't hurt?" Throughout the process I gained people but along the way I equally lose people including myself there for a while.

I had started relieving the same family cycles in my relationships, but that would only be because everything I ever learned was centered on toxicity. When it came to romantic relationships, I was the kingpin. Or at least, I always felt like it. These were in the days where I wanted to be just like my dad because if nobody knew nothing else, I had eyes, a dimple, and way with word that typically got me out of a lot of trouble but also into a lot of trouble. From girls at parties fighting over who was coming to my dorm that night to fellas making comments like "Dan Dan is the only girl I know that I wouldn't leave my girlfriend in a room with because she might not come back home." I had done it all.

Once, I had two people I was talking to at the same time. This particular evening, I was seated with both of them in the same space--I accidentally had them over at the same time. This would normally feel weird, but for me at this time, it wasn't. I knew my way around things like this and just what to do to handle the situation. I had one of the girls pretend that she was my relative. On a second occasion, it was with two of my exes. I had always known how uncomfortable they felt around each other and how much they disliked themselves, but it felt just right to convince them to be comfortable with all three of us being together. Sounded like a good idea right? Good times, right? It was far from that and at the age of 25, I knew poly relationships may not have been my thing.

You know, to me, love has never been a familiar term or feeling the way most people view love because our relationship has always been bittersweet. This unfamiliarity shaped me in my relationships, so much so that the one time I thought that I was starting to get a hang of what love really was, the relationship got destroyed by a monster that I had created in Brina. Everybody has a breaking point and despite the love she had for me eventually she gave me back everything I gave her like the perfect chess player. From there on, I couldn't never understand in the slightest bit, what love was or how to even express it properly. Love has always been something that I have feared. For most of my life, people scared me, and this was because my journey that far had taught me that love and hurt moved arm in arm. That, when someone loved you, they will hurt you, and because you wouldn't want to be alone, you would forgive them. Love looked like mental abuse, embarrassing jokes, humiliation, physical abuse, internalizing pain, accepting being gaslit, touching people inappropriately, and agreeing so you're not abandoned or shunned. My fear of abandonment kept me in a lot of situations that common sense and self-worth could've taken me out of. I remember vaguely dating one person, Kali, just because she had a name for herself. This was the worst relationship of my life for several of reason. Even years later the impact of that relationship affected my life. But ironically, this was one person out of the polygamy relationship I experienced.

In these days, I truly believed that every person that I had ever dated played side-line to my high school sweetheart Brina, because we could just never leave each other alone, even in college. No matter how many times I messed up or went through something she was there to pick up the pieces. Her works were doing unknowingly but she had enough respect for my feelings to keep it a secret where I on the other hand had no regards for anyone's feelings besides my own.

For most of my life, I believe I've had a tug a war with people in general, and this has pushed some genuine people away. However, I am always consoled by the advantage that this lifestyle brought. It had always weeded out who didn't need to be there—in my life. I devoted most of my life to adapting to people to survive and feel a sense of love to where eventually I lost my own identity. I know a lot of things I did in life came from wanting to belong, but losing myself was actually creating a monster of confusion and its name was rage.

Years in, I started to understand myself better and it brought different realms of realisation. This transition begun with a decision. The decision that I wanted more, that I was tired of living the way I did, in these cycles that had started to look the same. I was finally ready to give up just sitting and turn the doorknob into the light. While I would like to sound as if this decision was based solely on a light bulb moment I cannot because this came from a teachable moment. Again, being in heat of rage with Kali one night I was sent to jail. There's a cliché saying that most people talk about *"it's not what you know but who you know"* and I was about to see first hand how it works. As I sat there in that jail cell praying and crying the only thing, I could think about is the right decisions I could have made at the wrong time. While I panicked (again God acting on my behalf) little did I know that there was an officer that knew well that brought me in that advocated on my behalf. The was a jailer that came to my cell as I sat there in a state of fear smelling like coffee and a long night in the barn that yelled "Harper!" Me fearful of what was coming next, I responded "Yes." I hadn't realized that Sal the officer had discussed that I was in school and had no prior offenses but also knew the background of what actually happened. Upon being released that night with a promise to never be seen in jail or court again, this was when my life took a turn for the better.

    I remember when I finally started to making this change there were so many other things that started changing around me. I stopped smoking 5-10 blunts a day, was more to myself, my grades started improving, and I even attempted at having a conversation with my parents about how their life choices affected my present-day mind set. The irony of how even in the worst of situation, there's always something that you needed to learn for each moment even if the situation in present day is uncomfortable. You often have to be uncomfortable in order to shift and moved because if you weren't you would never move. Despite the way things happened in my college years both good and bad there are several of things that I accomplished. I gained two wonderful mentors that to date are still my biggest cheerleaders, I have earned 4 degrees and two of those being Master of Science degrees, I have joined two honor societies and a sorority, I later was licensed as a counsellor by the State of Arkansas to begin my career as a therapist from being a mental health paraprofessional, and I got a bunch of answers from my parents but a secret that would change my life in my 30's.

CHAPTER 5

WALKING IN YOUR TRUTH

"When you start your journey of healing, you begin to piece the pieces together for your peace." - AH

Before anything begins, there are two important questions that you need to ask yourself: **<u>What is your truth?</u>** What are those things you've secretly been running away from? What are those realities that you have successfully hidden behind a façade?

<u>What is a version of the truth that you tell yourself?</u> What do you often say to yourself to justify your actions, your being where you are, your decisions? What is the version of your story that you have told yourself?

Take a pause and reflect. Identifying the answers to this makes all the difference.

We lie to ourselves. We often spend the time convincing ourselves of what to believe; "I am this way because I grew up in a broken home", "I do not love because I wasn't shown how to", "I do not know these things because I didn't learn them." We would tell ourselves anything to trick our minds into thinking that it is okay. We'd do anything to survive, exist...anything to help us cope. We would fight so hard to justify our actions and decisions. We would rather do all these when deep down, we know that we cannot truly justify anything. People have been through worse and done better.

This is why telling yourself the truth is important. Transparency, as difficult and uncomfortable as it may be, is necessary for us if we want to live our lives, and not merely exist.

I started to learn this in the remaining parts of my college years but will only come into a new dispensation after college. My last years in college were filled with toxic relationships, ups and downs, and trial and error as the shift in my life began to take place. But of course, these were all part of life's lessons. During this time, me and Brina were constantly into it because secretly she had become me but she was a lot better at it simply because in my eyes she was the purest part about me. I remember when I first found out about her having other male and females that she conversed with it was a act of betrayal and loss that I don't think I ever came back from. Even outside of the back and forth with Brina, I often found myself going through the hardest of situations, mostly because I was still learning how to use my voice and express my emotions in the proper way (for most people my voice and emotions came off as anger and intimidation). I saw friendships and relationships blossom and wither, but I was learning. I was learning to stop hardening myself in an attempt to keep people from seeing the cracks that I had on the inside. Cracks can always be fixed, sealed, mended. I was cracked and broken. And even if I was, it is broken wood that makes furniture. I was learning to live above the imposter syndrome that had shrunk me to mediocrity. I struggled, constantly letting the inner critic in me make me feel like I didn't deserve happiness or any good thing. Self-sabotage had been my armoury--I could destroy myself before anything destroyed me or destroy others before they became a threat. But how long was this going to work for me?

At this point, I likened my story to going up a long flight of stairs. It often gets to a distance where you will need to take a pause to catch your breath. It is impulsive to want to bask in the relief of remaining there. The pain and discomfort try to prevent you from thinking about moving forward. But true joy and relief come from forging forward. When you make progress, you can look down and see how far you've come. Looking at the entire staircase can be overwhelming but when you learn to take it step by step. It leaves you with the anticipation of what the excitement will be when you arrive at your destination each time. For a change, I wanted to walk forward with joy.

After college, I continued in the heart-wrenching pattern of jumping from one relationship to another, but only because I desperately needed a place to stay as I had no one. There were several of hurts that paid the cost along the way for me to survive or even me learning myself that I knew would come with great remorse later in life. But then, the year 2017 suddenly became a pivotal year of my life. It marked the beginning of both heartbreak and healing—two contrasting emotions that would play a major role in bringing me into the wholesome light that I am walking in today.

The breakup was the first significant hurt that I had felt in a really long time. I mean, I was surrounded by the hurting reality of my life, but that was a wound that I had grown into seeing every day. This time, it was fresh…a new cut, an open wound. A breakup at that time would mean that I was no longer going to get the comforting benefit of a couch to sleep on and wondering where I would sleep at from day to day. College was over, life was going to hit me like a freight train. Not now, when I was trying to forge forward. Why was everything falling apart?

I got to realize that perhaps, life did this to steer me on to the right part of healing, and this realization gave me my answers. I was trying to do it on my own before. Chances are that I probably wouldn't have come this far if I was still on that path. Life was breaking me to forge me again into the woman I was going to become.

This journey started in a quaint little coffee shop that I had found comfort in during these years. See in these years I had went back to being homeless and couch hoping again where I couldn't see past this will be my forever. I sat there, staring at my untouched cup of hot chocolate, lost in the thoughts of the pain my heart had been feeling. The room buzzed with conversations, but in my mind, there was only a deafening silence that came from absolute loneliness. By chance--or as it was intentionally pre-ordained by the universe, I stumbled on a therapeutic foster care group. Something about it made me think of my life and what it had been so far, what it would have been if I had foster care and therapy all in one place. I considered the children lucky. Privileged enough to have something I didn't, something that I slowly began to see that I needed. The thoughts of getting therapy stayed on my mind for long, becoming more pressing each day than it was on the day before. Soon, I made the decision that I was going to give therapy a shot. I had a problem, I was a mess, but again, I was going to do anything that I could to stop feeling that way.

I walked into a Dr. Jay's office that day feeling like I had just stepped into a new light. I had been to therapy before, long time ago but didn't quite stick around for long. Something about this time felt absolutely different.

Dr. Jay was a lovely woman. Not only was she beautiful on the outside, but she also had a comforting personality that I could sense from the moment that I walked in through her door. She was one of the professionals behind the therapeutic foster care that I had discovered before, so being in her office this day made perfect sense.

It was surprisingly cozy; a comfy couch, a soft warm light, and a box of tissues that sat on the side table. There was an initial hesitation when I first took a seat in the room, but then, the woman stared at me with eyes that threatened to peer through my soul, and I couldn't help but let my guard down.

"Have you had this experience before. Therapy?"

I nodded a yes to her question. She needed to know that I had been through EMDR training before. Eye Movement Desensitization and Reprocessing (EMDR) is a psychotherapy that enables people to heal from the symptoms and emotional distress that are the result of disturbing life experiences. It is a distinct therapeutic approach which uses bilateral stimulation (of which eye movements can be an example) to aid the processing of distressing information. EMDR is commonly used to treat post-traumatic stress disorder (PTSD). It is now increasingly being used to treated other conditions in which disturbing memories play a part.

I saw a safe place to pour my heart out, my fears for once. And for the first time in a long while, I felt like someone actually listened to me and I was giving a microphone to my shame, guilt, and pain. On that day and every other day afterward, I was heard but also, I was learning for the first time. I was all over the place with my thoughts and emotions, but Dr. Jay was patient. She would always smile and tell me that had the tools all along, and I just needed to learn how to use them. Now, she was teaching me.

I found emotions to focus on, grief and loss. It occurred to me that I had deposits of grief and loss that I hadn't addressed or even thought of. Throughout my life I had experienced loss, but I didn't recognize it. It brings to acknowledging the truth that you can never truly fix a problem if you do not know what the problem is in the first place. I didn't know what loss was--everything seemed normal to me. So how was I going to heal from it? From every standpoint, I was in loss, loss of trust, loss of safety, loss of protection, loss of love, and a loss of self. Then I realized, all the weight I had been carrying for all these years slowly being lifted. Therapy was working, and I realized that it wasn't about fixing what was broken, but learning to drop the weights to heal, and carrying its scars with strength.

Needless to say, my life took a drastic turn under Dr. Tori's amazing influence. In the company of professionals who understood the labyrinth of the human mind, I discovered the power of resilience. Friendships blossomed, providing a support system I had never known. For once I wasn't forging trauma bonds where we only connected through pain but forming healthy connections with people that wanted to heal. Through the haze of despair, I began to learn mental and behavioral health techniques that not only mended my own wounds but equipped me to guide others on a similar journey. Dr. Jay gave me everything I needed, and I was then introduced to another great therapist that began my career. Michelle a social worker, was the first person that gave me the chance to care for kids under her care, as well as the other professionals she worked with. It was there I met Grace, an adorable kid that left a striking mark in my heart right from the first day.

Grace's story was similar to mine, like Dr. Jay had often told me. She came from a mother that wasn't perfect and was struggling to learn how to be a parent. It's funny how we always say kids don't come with instructions, but we miss the fact that parents don't either. Tralla was Grace's mother, and everyone was working with her in order to make reunite her and Grace but for now I would watch over and guide her until her mother learned love. But this is not what formed the basis of my fondness for her. The little girl was an incredibly smart and cheerful soul. Grace could never let me catch a breather. I didn't realize that this happiness was what I needed to heal, until she came into my life. In her eyes, I saw reflections of my own struggles and triumphs. This child, seemingly fragile yet resilient, became the beacon of change I needed. I was suddenly filled with the urge to protect Grace from everything I had been through, to have a child of my own, and to cater for every other child that may be facing the same struggles. Here, my career was born. I embraced the role of a teacher and guide, standing on the line between being the healer and being healed. These children, with their scars and stories, became my inspiration. In their presence, I found the strength to confront my past and reimagine my future.

CHAPTER 6

THE NEW DESTINATION

"No matter the place; where we started from is not our final destination, unless we make it so" – **AH**

If there is one important lesson that I have learned throughout my journey, it will be that: The goal is not to be perfect, but to keep learning how to get better every day. Everything that you experience in life is a learning experience that produces boundaries and standards in your life.

Therapy taught me everything I needed to learn for the next phase of my journey. I was enlightened on Post Traumatic Stress Disorder (PTSD)-- the mental health condition that's triggered by a terrifying event, either by experiencing it or witnessing it. I learned the symptoms:

Reliving flashbacks, paranoia, hallucinations, and nightmares of the incident. Avoiding as, avoiding people, places, things, or memories that remind the trauma. Excessive arousal as increased alertness, anger, fits of rage, irritability, or hatred, difficulty sleeping or concentrating. Intrusive negative distressing thoughts or feelings such as guilt, and Delays in motor skills or language, amongst others.

I identified my triggers; what they were and where they were in, and Dr. amazing Jay handed me several books that helped me along the way. I remember a couple of them; Brene Brown's *"Atlas of the Heart"* and *"The Grief Recovery Handbook"* by John W. James et al.

A free marketing for two amazing books.

The older Danielle Jones was taking responsibility for who she was and not pinning it on some generational curse or her life's circumstances. The actions of the older Danielle Jones were driven by wholesome therapy. The older Danielle Jones was starting to realize that all this while, her actions were only symbolic. Her inner child had been screaming to be heard, yet without a voice. I hadn't healed to be a space safe enough for her. Therapy taught me to give my emotions a voice. To give younger Danielle this voice that she had been missing. I was starting to understand that loss is a part of life. The grief book redefined grief to me as an emotion that shows what we need a person or situation to be for us, one more time. I learned to honor my feelings. I had always experienced love, contrary to what you may think. Only, I had seen both the healthy and unhealthy versions of it. So, to say, I have always experienced unconditional love from my family. Bad ways, or ways that I do not agree with, do not equal bad people. They are just what they are; bad ways that I do not agree with. In essence, my family's actions do not make them bad people. I learned to forgive, and the first person I ever genuinely forgave was my mother.

During this time, she was admitted into the hospital for a life-threatening health scare. She was septic. I remember rushing her to the hospital that night with the fear that I was going to lose her. She was rushed straight into the emergency unit and scheduled for an emergency surgery. Dealing with my mother's condition and also struggling with the mistrust I had was extremely challenging. I was also diagnosed with stage one cervical cancer during this time. Anxiety crippled me, and the fear of what was to come totally overwhelmed my being. I was all she had, and even though I had been hurt countless times by her, I still had to be there for her---and quite frankly, for myself as well. During these times and since he was 19, Airen stayed in and out of the jail due to becoming the person that hurt him. I don't think my brother ever healed from his innocence being stolen and began to inflict that same pain on to others. I think during this time I was drove me the most because despite her health declining the only thing, she worried about was sending him money to get on his books weekly. 25 dollars every week for 10+ years can be costly, but I never understood how she did it because only had a 725-dollar SSI check monthly.

People asked a lot of questions—questions I had no answer to at my young age. They wanted to know what was going on, how I was going to handle it, what the doctors were doing, and every other question they shouldn't have been asking me. We didn't have a lot of health professionals at our disposal besides a nurse, Tia that I met along the way that I trusted her professional opinion. During this time, I would call her often out of fear and ask her things but I was thankful because I didn't exactly deal her the best hand during our time. Everyone calling and asking question about her care was a high cost for me and it wasn't something that I could easily afford. Because all the question marks only made my anxiety worse which was a high cost to pay.

Worse still, my mother came out of surgery needing a ventilator. She couldn't breathe on her own. Things got scarier and even more debilitating. Somewhere at the back of my mind, I was hit with the constant memories of how she left me for dead all the times that I had needed her. All the times I wanted her to show up and be my life support. Now she needed one?

I consented to letting her be put on vent. It was a big decision, and a painful one. But my heart wasn't hardened enough to let my mother go when I knew that I had the chance to save her. I wasn't her. I wanted to be more.

For four days, I terrifyingly watched my mother battle for her life with a ventilator. She finally snatched it out on the fifth day—a way to tell me that she was still fighting. But what should have been a relieving day, soon became a momental period in my life. A few hours after she was back to being herself, my mother took on her habitual ways and wore it on like a cloak.

"Why did you not pay the phone bill?" "Why haven't you checked my mail?" "Do I have to ask you to do that?'

She was fussing about every single thing. So much that I was forced to think that it was her condition. But it was not! This was just who my mother really was.

It was nerve racking; she had just gotten out of coma, and off life support after a decision I had made to keep her alive, even in my own condition. Impulsively that day, right there, I broke down in tears.

It was in that moment I knew that I was truly changing. The old Danielle would have put up an attitude and walk away.

"Now why are you crying?" My mother gave the most insensitive reaction to my emotional state.

I sniffed, with my voice slightly raised "Do you not realize what happened to you?" I was extremely curious. Was she just choosing to be intentionally oblivious, or was she really clueless?

She looked at me in an uproar "What?" she asked.

"Life support! You just came off it. How can your mail and phone bill be all you care about?" I was infuriated. "Can you for once consider that I am your youngest child, and I had to be faced with the difficulty of making this decision that concerned your life?"

"Why does that bother you? You did what I would have asked you to if I could speak?" she grew more insensitive with each response.

"I've been here before, mom," I continued "...in a position where you had the chance to save me, but instead you walked away. then, and every other time after. You left me to fight for myself but when the shoe was placed on the other foot, I didn't return to you what you gave me. You always come down on me so hard about the slightest thing, but when I had the opportunity, I fought keep you here. I walked a mile for every day you were in a coma praying that my steps and energy would bring just as many breaths to your body so you could breathe on your own. I was frightened every day to see you lay there with a machine breathing life into you and the only thing you can do is fuss at me for what I didn't do?"

This day became a turning point for my mother and I in our relationship. I didn't always like everything that she did, but I had learned to meet her where she was in life. I've learned self-love and unconditional positive regard for myself as well as others. I learned what it was like to fall in love for the first time, and to also experience commitment from a partner by simply being myself. Just because I had experienced pain all my life, didn't mean that I was difficult to love. I also deserved good things, and I was willing to go for it.

****

In a sequence of things, as time went own surrounding my brother getting out of jail, me and my mother exchanged words. "Why do I have to watch you be ran to a grave loving a child that only loves himself!" was the last argument we had in April. Not knowing in between time my mother had suspicion that she was about to pass away and called upon her best friend, Aunt Joe Ann. "Joe Ann, I know Danielle is going to be okay, but its Airen that I worry about. I have to get it right with my children before I leave her especially Danielle because she deserves to know." It was first mentioned to me by my dad when is was 21 that there was a possibility that my dad wasn't my dad but at that time I was young and didn't want the truth. I found out my mother's long-held secret three weeks before she passed, and she confirmed; My father may have not been my biological father. My mother had let it out, all of it. And before she left, she had tried to make it right even when I refused it. I guess that she was hit with the realization that it was the only chance she had left to make it right. She called me on a Saturday night, and I was drunk in a parking lot crying when my phone rang. On the other side her voice as calm as could be said "I didn't call you to argue with you I just wanted to call and check on you because I felt you heavy in my spirt." In anger I responded, "It's a fine time to have a fucking mother's intuition!" and then I hung up. She texted me "I didn't call to argue with you, but I do understand that you are hurt, and I am here to talk when you are ready." But I was already at peace or so I thought anyways. You see I didn't answer that text back that night and my mother passed away the following Tuesday night. It took a part of me to heal, and I should have realized it sooner; my mother couldn't give me more than she had to give. Healing is a choice that everyone doesn't make, but she did take a swing at healing our relationship before she passed away. That day, I sat in the room, and I cried, holding tightly onto her hands. For hours, the only thing that I could manage in response to her last words was that I was sorry too. Yet, she couldn't hear it. I let it all go when I let go of her hand. During before the time of planning a funeral I was full of anger and hurt to where I regretfully fought my brother Airen soon after my mother's funeral. When I closed the lid of her casket for the last time at her funeral, I knew I had to forgive her in order to find peace for myself, and with her permanent absence from my life.

 I was sorry; it was in this event that I realized that I truly healed from every emotional abuse that I was subjected and had subjected myself to. Truthfully, I had some point in my life, truly believed that

I was a narcissist. "I'm sorry" wasn't a common phrase that I used only because I was taught not to be unless I gained from it. I had always believed that it was a sign of weakness. That it made me inferior and all I ever wanted to have was a superior sense of entitlement. "I'm sorry" to me, was only a ploy to frighten me into domination, a statement made only because I was seeking to be loved. But I saw that I was starting to care about others more than I cared about myself. That I cared enough to admit that I was sorry without fearing anything.

From having my grandparents (my grandmother passed away a year later) and mother pass away, I have grown to not only value myself, but also to value people more because truly, no one lasts for ever. Even memories aren't exactly for a lifetime. You see, the 'monsters that I called family' were never really monsters. Just like I was, they were broken children who never found freedom from the cage that they had been in the past. They were children surviving with no escape, Danielles that never saw the light, people who never knew what it felt like to heal from trauma.

Perhaps, they would have done better if they knew better. I could never truly blame them for their actions. We are an embodiment of all the things we have learned. Only, some other people intentionally choose to unlearn.

My story has made me a better person even as I continue to tell it to others that are willing to listen. But looking back at the stories of the ones who had gone before me, I become proud of where I have come from. My story began with tracing a generational curse to its root, but it ends with cursing the curse by taking those life experience to save others as well as myself even my family. It ends with the miracle child who chose to be herself and not her family or what her family had made. I have gained more than I ever lost in love, friendships, a healthier family, and learning to give/receive healthy love. I have purchased a home, I have two vehicles, a private practice, and so much more but my best accomplishment in life will be learning love. Along the way I learned that it's okay to let other people love you and to properly love others. All help doesn't hurt, and all hurt isn't to break you but rather for you to learn. I once had someone tell me "You're not hard to love." And that was life changing for me with that moment because I think those words are what I had been searching high and low for in life. At times we get so used to telling that bad things that happen in life because we want to emotionally grab people to where we miss that positive things attract healthy people too. You don't have to survive, exist, but you can live, and I mean truly live.

Do I have it all now? No

Have I attained perfection? No

Do I have what it takes to give you 'a life manual'? No

But do I find telling my storey a necessity? I do, always.

For some of you, by picking this book, you have found a story that resonates with yours. If by any chance this speaks to you, I hope this serves as a reminder that you are not on your own. I hope that as you read through the remaining lines of this book, you are brought into the light that you too can begin your journey of healing at any moment. That you too can chose to end that curse, be different, fight for who you are, learn your identity. That moment when you close this book and stare at your own reflection, your healing has began. Hold on to it. In reality, healing doesn't always look like a chapter of a book. Healing takes time, long processes even but is not linear. But it is important that you do not look at the entire staircase and get wearied out. Take one step at a time. Always remember; ***the goal is not perfection. The goal is to get better every day and learn. There's no such thing as a lost cause only a work in progress.***

Welcome to the light, dear miracle child!

ABOUT THE AUTHOR

By Arial Harper

They say that you are a product of your environment but when she couldn't change her environment, she changed herself which shifted her environment. Arial Daniyelle Harper is a Licensed Professional Counselor, a writer, a public speaker, and panellist originally from Southwest Arkansas. She has an associate degree in Psychology, bachelor's degree in psychology with a minor in Criminal Justice, a master's degree in Human Services, and a master's degree in Clinical Mental Health and Counseling from Southern Arkansas University. From becoming a behavioral specialist to a qualified behavioral health professional, she began her career towards becoming a licensed Therapist but her life experience with trauma, grief, and other mental health issues birthed her into a career unknowingly. She is a member of Zeta Phi Beta Sorority Incorporated, Alpha Chi and a member of the advisory board for the Law School at the University of Arkansas in Fayetteville LGBTQ+ community. She currently resides in Central Arkansas where she is the Founder and Operator of C.O.P. OUT, LLC (Children of Purpose Outreach) for therapeutic services ranging from depression to childhood trauma with specialties in grief/loss, trauma, and Eye Movement Desensitization Reprocessing (EMDR). Miracle Child is her first book; an unpublished story now being told. *"Broken wood makes furniture too."*- **Arial. H**

This is something that Arial lives by and the gift of hope that she aims to give through her life's worth as a therapist and through this book. By the end I charge you to be the fire that guides on torch rather than a fire to destroy because every way you get to choose rather you are a passenger or driver of life.

Milton Keynes UK
Ingram Content Group UK Ltd.
UKHW052245220424
441436UK00007BA/53